EXPERIMENTING WITH GOD
In Families And Schools

**Miracle Blessings that come from obeying Him
through Scripture and His Modern Messenger**

Raymond and Dorothy Moore

**Edited by a Moore Foundation team of Raymond and Dorothy Moore,
Cris Carver, Emileen Denney, Jessica Meissner and Chris Price.**

Cover by Amy Wetmore and graphics artist Jessica Meissner

**Box 1
Camas, WA 98607
Conversation phone: (360) 835-5500**

**Website: moorefoundation.com
E-Mail: moorefnd@pacifier.com**

The Soul Of A Child

The soul of a child is the loveliest flower
That grows in the Garden of God.
Its climb is from weakness to knowledge and power
To the sky from the clay to the clod.
To beauty and sweetness it grows under care.
Neglected, 'tis ragged and wild.
'Tis a plant that is tender, but wondrously rare.
The sweet wistful soul of a child.

Be tender, O gardner, and give it its share
Of moisture, of warmth and of light,
And let it not lack for the painstaking care
To protect it from frost and from blight.
A glad day will come when its bloom shall unfold,
It will seem that an Angel has smiled
Reflecting a beauty and sweetness untold
In the sensitive soul of a child.

Anon.

EXPERIMENTING WITH GOD

TABLE OF CONTENTS

PARTIAL ABBREVIATION LIST OF ELLEN WHITE'S BOOKS

Key	Book Title
AA	The Acts of the Apostles
AH	The Adventist Home
1BC	The Seventh-day Adventist Bible Commentary, vol. 1 (2BC etc., for vols 2-7)
CD	Counsels on Diet and Foods
CG	Child Guidance
CH	Counsels on Health
COL	Christ's Object Lessons
CS	Counsels on Stewardship
CT	Counsels to Parents, Teachers, and Students.
DA	The Desire of Ages
Ed	Education
Ev	Evangelism
EW	Early Writings
FE	Fundamentals of Christian Education
GC	The Great Controversy
GW	Gospel Workers
LS	Life Sketches of Ellen G. White
MB	Thoughts From the Mount of Blessing
MH	The Ministry of Healing
MM	Medical Ministry
MYP	Messages to Young People
PK	Prophets and Kings
SC	Steps to Christ
SD	Sons and Daughters of God
SL	The Sanctified Life
1SM	Selected Messages, book 1
2SM	Selected Messages, book 2
SR	The Story of Redemption
1T	Testimonies, vol. 1 (2T etc., for vols. 2-9)
TM	Testimonies to Ministers and Gospel Workers

Once to every man and nation comes the moment to decide,
In the strife of Truth with Falsehood for the good or evil side.
Truth forever on the scaffold, Wrong forever on the throne.
Then it is the brave man chooses while the coward stands aside.
Doubting in his object spirit till his Lord is crucified.

—James Russell Lowell

P R O L O G U E

OUR CHURCH'S UNIQUENESS--
WHAT GOOD IS A PROPHET?

Backdrop. *When Dorothy and I lived at Pacific Union College, we exchanged fruit with our neighbors. They liked our Gravenstein apple trees, and we were occasionally their garden guests. But we didn't know the hazards. Nor did they, or they would have warned us. One day I was picking big black youngberries for Dorothy, when a small branch at the top of the vine moved strangely. On closer look, I saw that the "branch" was a tiny rattlesnake, the same color and size as the branches, feeding on a berry inches from my fingers. What if I hadn't looked? What if...?*

What if you had a physician who let you continue with a medicine that he knew had side effects that may lead to paralysis or death? Or what if a friend **had truth** *that had eternal consequences but was afraid that it would interfere with your lifestyle or confront you with deep-seated prejudices on your job or in your Church? Or how about* **your** *accountability? What do* **you** *do as a church member about God-given* **truths** *through Scripture or Ellen White [EGW] that are overlooked or ignored in your hospital or school, yet hold a key to immediate and eternal goals? What would you write in your book if after years of blessings, God tells you to "Arise, shine...Cry aloud....enlarge... spare not, lengthen thy cords, and strengthen thy stakes...?"[Isa 54, 58, 60] We face such tests in this book. [See also Eze. 3: 20-21;DA 441]*

Wonderful things are happening. Our overseas divisions are setting a blistering pace. Many of our youth are far ahead of us adults. Yet many schools have inherited trends of the past. At this writing, a leading union conference educational director estimates that at least 99% of North American SDA schools fail to follow EGW's crucial instruction for teachers to mentor their students in daily manual work at least half the school day. Our Chapters 8 to 10 will show that some conventional policies amount to child abuse which deprives youth of creative potential and the blessings God guarantees when we diligently obey. Many homes and schools have mistaken their values. Over the last 25 years, we have replicated more than 50 times a brief study of children at the transition ages of 11 to 15.

GOD'S THERAPY FOR FAMILIES AND SCHOOLS

First, the promises: Below are our explicit guides providing God's timely blessings for 60 years around the world.

OUR INSPIRATION

"I will send you Elijah the prophet before...the great and dreadful day of the Lord; and he shall turn the heart of the fathers (parents) to the children, and the heart of the children to their fathers..." Malachi 4:5,6

OUR PHILOSOPHY

From Scripture: *"If you diligently obey the voice of the Lord, your God, to observe carefully all His commandments which I comman you today—[He] will set you above all nations...And all these blessings shall come upon you and overtake you if you obey the voice of the Lord your God...[He] will make you the head an not the tail, above only and not beneath.*

"Arise, shine, for your light has come... Gentiles shall come to your light, and kings to your rising... Foreigners will rebuild your walls...bring you the wealth of the nations...kings shall minister unto you... Lengthen your cords and strengthen your stakes. For you shall expand to the right and to the left... Do not fear...you will not be ashamed."

"Teach...diligently unto they children...when thou sittest in thy house...walkest by the way...liest down...risest up." Deut 28, 6:6,7; Isaiah 60, 54 NKJV

From Ellen White: *"Children should virtually be trained in a homeschool until maturity." Child Guidance 26-7—[i.e. close to parents, but if you can't do that]"place your children in training schools where the influences are similar to those of a rightly conducted home school." Testimonies, Vol. 8 [8T] 226.*

"Our teachers should not think that their work ends with giving instruction from books. Several hours each day should be devoted to working with the students in some line of manual training. In no case should this be neglected." Counsels to Parents, Teachers and Students, 211. [TO SAN FERNANDO SCHOOL—JUNIOR COLLEGE WHICH PREPARED PREMEDICAL STUDENTS FOR CME IN Medical Ministry 81, ETC.]

"If the youth can have but a one sided-education, which is of the greater consequence, a knowledge of the sciences, with all the disadvantages of life and health, or a knowledge of labor for practical life. We unhesitatingly answer, the latter. If one must be neglected, let it be the study of books." Fundamentals of Christian Education, [FCE 41].

"The amusements [including rivalry sports] are doing more to counteract the working of the Holy Spirit than anything else, and the Lord is grieved." FCE 220-28, CT 348 [TO ALL SCHOOLS]

"Though in many respects our Institutions of learning have swung into worldly conformity...they are prisoners of hope. If they listen to His voice and follow His ways, God will correct and enlighten them, and bring them back to their upright position of distinction from the world." 6T 145

Our goal was to determine their *real* preferences for long-term happiness. In Chapter 17 we offer details, with results and implications.

It is crucial that all of us insure our living the values which our staffs, patients and students should have. It is abusive to replace God-designed health and education with expedient programs of health care and of TV and sports, which EGW says are distracting from the King's coming, counteracting the Holy Spirit [Matt 24:37-39, FE221].

We write to tell you principles and methods proven from EGW and sound research and practice, yet they are not widely known in the Church, and Chapter 2 tells a possible reason why. How about a stinging Serpent who distracts from God's EGW instructions? He is far more menacing than the little green intruder on our neighbors' vine. We want to get the message to all before their fingers are stung by the Serpent, or tell them where to find the antidote if they are already bitten.

If you read the box on page 2, you found why, from our experience, we write this, and you will see how eager God is to heal and to bless. For example, do you know God's creative secrets on debt freedom for families and schools? on discipline of discipleship? On how to develop more mature reasoning earlier in children? Have you tried God's research and Inspiration-based recipe for making kings out of kids who don't realize that they are born to the Palace...in Heaven?

Solutions. Last year our two lay/professional teams did this again. They have opened and are operating ten Church schools their conferences or missions closed, but are now open and debt-free. They have initiated joint teacher-student balanced work-study-service plans tailored as much as possible to each child's readiness, interests, aptitudes, and abilities. God has blessed as He promises, if we obey.

When you review the box on the previous page, do remember that Jesus is closing His Books for eternity! He has mapped directions to His throne room. [Rev3:20-21] He went to infinite pains to send and arm His messenger. Her authenticity is sometimes vouched for more strongly by eminent scientists and statesmen than by most of us and our leaders. [Chapters 13 to 16] He allows not a breath of sin through those gates—nothing His grace cannot cover.

Our goals here for individuals and institutions. We share with all families and schools the sound research principles and methods God has given to change rebels into champions for Him, and turn students lost in sports and amusements into industrious godly workers who know how to earn a living as well as how to shoot a basket. Such families enjoy togetherness, and such teachers savor blessings that He promises if we *diligently* obey. [Deut 28] Their schools increase enrollments, accelerate achievement and reduce costs. Students win scholarships, families enjoy health. *But above all, they develop noble, creative, Godly characters for lives that measure with the Life of God.* [SDG p.365]

Questions? His blessings may seem exaggerated as we tell them. So, on reading this book, if you have questions of any kind, hold us to account for sound evidence. In this book you will find that work, study and service methods are practical for both home and school. When adults use older students to help the younger, and the stronger to help the weaker, every child may have sound personal care. [ED285-6] God is *anxious* to make us "the head and not the tail...above only and not beneath." But we must give Him a chance!

For 63 years at every occasion imaginable, we have had questions tipped, tossed or thrown at us about God's counsel through Scripture, Ellen White and research: at church, dinners, seminars, on planes, TV/radio, Internet, television and even telephone (an information operator and a Gallup pollster). We have watched or listened in awe as sheer curiosity became sincere concern and openness for truth which God has showered on us in America and overseas.

Adventists have always been welcome to our joint Research/EGW family and school seminars, public lectures and church sermons. Yet in North America over the last 30 years most sessions have been arranged by other churches or secular groups. Our God-inspired prophet, Ellen White, meets all the Bible standards and is honored by the scrutiny of secular scholars. Quite a few are quoted in this book. *Don't forget this treasure, lest we reap Israel's curses for rejecting her prophets.* (**Israel had second chances. We will not. Time is ending. Eternity is almost here.**) *God offers only one eternity. Thank you, Father. We must not fail to study thoroughly His clear maps, written in the language, mood and detail of our times by His messenger, Ellen White, inspired by the same Holy Spirit who spoke to the Bible prophets.*

Since He has the answers, our *Malachi Movement* master seminars use His Scriptural, EGW writings and sound research to train teams as seminar leaders who in turn train others. It was to share her answers with firm support of the best in family and child development research that prompted this book. *We repeat, research that backs EGW's message is cherished across America, yet is not well known among Adventists, as it should be if they are to carry it to others.* More on this in Chapters 8 and 9.

So we set out under God in behalf of all creeds to review the largely -overlooked or rejected preventive and healing process we describe here and lay down in the box on page two. We remind you that *God gave it to EGW for us today:* He told Israel, *"...them that honor me, I will honor"* [1 Samuel 2:30 KJV]. He had EGW tell us in endtimes that *"With us, as with Israel of old, success in education depends on fidelity in carrying out the Creator's plan."* [ED 50]

Our principal focus is on several of the Church's most urgent needs: (1) Establishing the primacy of the home in children's lives. (2) Confirming the crucial place of God's joint parent- and teacher-student balanced work-study-service program both at home and in school. (3) Helping schools in areas that are often neglected. (4) Providing EGW's God-sent counsel on areas—diet, dress and adornment, health, music, social standards, sports, etc. We do this to *inform*. We do not claim to *reform*. That is the Holy Spirit's work. Failure to *diligently* obey God's endtimes warnings will cost us eternity. The task is not trouble-free, yet God guarantees it. His debt-free, creative, high achievement awards are thrilling. Try Him!

We offer you actual experiences of it—to grasp the Hand of God and experiment with Him. *The results can't honestly be credited any other way.* Replicable research from leading scholars confirms Him. EGW is upheld by research—eminent secular authorities and experiences that unveil God's simple ways to solve man's biggest problems.

God's initiation. You cannot avoid positive or negative personal publicity in or out of the Church if you do exactly what God says. For example, we are both praised and blamed as grandparents of the homeschool movement which echoes America's high literacy of two or three centuries ago. **God did it.** We had no idea, for example, that our *Harper's* article on the "Dangers of Early Schooling" was picked up by *Reader's Digest* until *after* it was published around the world. *God did this, not Moores.* **He inspired us through Scripture and Ellen White.**

He also initiated our book writing for Reader's Digest Press. Then He had an Adventist pastor's wife hand a copy of the book to Dr. James Dobson. This in turn changed Dr. Dobson's mind on early schooling. He has brought us to his program 21 times over 15 years and still mentions us. He even got us started on Thomas Nelson and Word Publishers. God arranged most of over 60 books that we authored or shared, including 35 or so university textbooks ranging from Columbia to Arizona State Universities. Church presses—Review, Pacific Press and three oriental presses published seven books over the last 50 years. Nearly all newspaper articles were initiated by news syndicates or such papers as *USA Today, Washington Post, Atlantic Constitution, Chicago Tribune, Arizona Republic, New York Times, Los Angeles Times* and other professional or popular journals. TV-Radio from TODAY, DONAHUE (2), OPRAH, VOP, AWR and 3ABN's two weekly programs for most of 15 years, number in thousands over 30 years.

Exactly how does this happen? We simply do what any ordinary mind can do. Study our favorite promises like Psalm 91, Proverbs 3:6 and Isaiah 26:3. We daily claim Deuteronomy 28:1,2, 13 which Elder Wilton Baldwin cited when we faced impossible human odds in Japan. (Please forgive us if we seem to overuse it. It has been the test that has opened miracle after miracle after miracle for 50 years.) We knew God had sent us (Chapter 6). We used Moses' words to Israel in every crisis, and often we have combined it with *Education*, page 50 by Ellen White: "With us, as with Israel of old, success in education depends on fidelity in carrying out the Creator's plan."

5

The years teach much
that the days never know.
—Ralph Waldo Emerson

CHAPTER 1

HOW WE HAPPENED TO EXPERIMENT WITH GOD
THROUGH ELLEN WHITE

Backdrop. *In the mid 1930s on the Pacific Union College Campus, I admired Dorothy Nelson as a fine, disciplined leader. I sat near her in a college class, but gave little special attention to any co-ed. I had neither the time, money nor clothes to be involved with anyone socially. I seldom had a full stomach, and regularly repaired my shoe soles with thick cardboard. But I'll never forget my one good shirt, starched and ironed to perfection, as Dorothy did with every shirt—like a millionaire's.*

Dorothy didn't have to work, yet she did. She spent much more of her time with less-privileged young women. Enrolled as a Methodist, Dorothy was baptized as a Seventh-day Adventist her first year at PUC, especially thrilled by Scripture and what she read from Ellen White [EGW] about Jesus, and about all-round lifestyles, and details about endtimes.

At PUC we were graced with teachers devoted to God's Word and EGW writings. Dorothy quickly noted that Mrs. White insisted that everything she wrote must be measured by the Bible. The wisdom of her articles and the certainty of her prophetic books convinced Dorothy that she was inspired by the same Holy Spirit as the Bible prophets. Later we will give you examples of world-class secular leaders who agree. Dorothy studied EGW education and health books hungrily. To the surprise of none who really knew her, she soon became a vegetarian, and later a vegan.

On the other hand, I had little time for unassigned reading and was relatively indifferent to matters of diet and Ellen White. I had enough problems in those Great Depression years just to survive. I was indeed down at the heels. But my apathy ebbed one day during Dorothy's last year, when out of the blue my roommate, Milton Maxwell, insisted I had a chance at winning the girl he called "the queen of the campus." Then, after a group social occasion one evening in the College Gymnasium where we went unattached, she asked how I'd like to be a vegetarian. I didn't know at the time that she was turning away from suitors who weren't interested in giving up their steaks and coffee. Nor was my answer a matter of principle: I wanted the girl! Quickly I replied, "I'd love to be a vegetarian." A year later we were married, and with that came a mutual devotion to Ellen White and my ardor for a classy vegetarian cook.

Experimenting with God. In our 86th year as I write this—the 64th of our marriage, and 67th and 68th years respectively of our teaching careers—Dorothy and I have found that Mrs. White's Spirit of Prophecy books, if followed diligently, are a simple, practical, low cost, no-fail formula for families, schools, sound health and character development at all levels. You will see why as you read this book. It has been demonstrated to unnumbered millions through the educational movement that EGW inspired, under God, the largest successful school movement in America, and perhaps the world. It was a modern version of Old-American home education. [See Chapter 9 "God's Great Educational Answer"] God's genius is full of wonders. His solutions are balanced, natural, true, and beautifully and logically-stated in words that are pure, kind and true, "an outward expression of an inward grace."

From the first weeks of our marriage, Dorothy and I agreed to test EGW counsel. So here we tell the years of miracles we have shared from God through her. Two anxieties weigh especially heavily on our hearts: (1) Our parent-education seminars here and abroad seldom pass without news about schools closing, and (2) abused or hurting children and families. EGW often highlights the needs of teamwork between families and schools. We have discovered that the only worthy answer is to experiment with God on His terms. His invitation is an incredible honor. So don't be surprised as you read on about a chain of miracles and how we know God led and keeps His promises!

God's management system. Our chain of blessings through Ellen White began in 1938 when, newly married, we settled as two public school teachers in a tiny Artesia, California "court" apartment. We had three goals—buy a new car, build a new house and obtain master's degrees. But we were sobered when a Godly physician, Dr. Claude Steen, and a business friend, came to our church from nearby Fullerton and talked about God's systematic benevolence plan. The Bible was his base, but he used EGW's inspired counsel to "Give at least a second tithe" like Israel did when they were en route to Canaan. "After all," he added, "we are headed for heavenly Canaan!" So there, we thought, had to go our new car, house and degrees! But God promised blessings, and said "Prove Me," so we started our life journey of faith.

With awe and a growing faith in experimenting with God, Scripture and Ellen White, we suddenly realized two years later what God had done: We had our new car, had built a model house, and both of us were well started on our master's degrees. Thus began a lifetime of faith and obedience, that Dorothy sparked at PUC, except of course the times when I occasionally ran ahead of God. Testing Him is exciting, and as it turned out, has always made uncommonly good sense. Now as we near the close of our lives on this earth, we need little of its goods anyway.

Some of these experiences are hard to explain. For example, I soon found that Dorothy was unusually frugal, so I always turned my check over to her.

7

We discovered also that God led us to remarkably good bargains in food and clothing. Yet we always ate well and had good clothes, although we admittedly bought a good deal of them from church rummage sales in well-to-do areas of town and from second-hand "boutiques." And we discovered while I was vice-president of Loma Linda University that our monthly food bill was half that of a neighbor's with the same-size family.

When we purchased houses or land, we also selected quality locations with views of creeks or lakes, if possible. The principle here is often and clearly stated by Ellen White. We always committed the situations to God and He proved to be an astonishingly brilliant Real Estate Agent. Our family has repeatedly raised the selling price when realtors thought the amount was too high. We then sold quickly, after telling the realtors "We'll let God sell it."

We started small, with the tithe, but the very experiment of testing God was exciting. And later when I was called to lead or share leadership in debt-ridden colleges, God always lifted us from Satan's money pits, and always produced debt freedom. His pockets, we have found, are *very* deep. Try Him! Experiment with Him! But only with diligent obedience to His Scripture and His modern messenger.

I lift my eyes to the Hills of God
Whose Hands caress the sky.
While near their breasts, His creatures stir
Its trees with psalm and sigh.

I stand, head bowed, midst His lofty peaks
Whose ears hear Nature's prayer:
The call of the fawn in the threat'ning storm,
Assurance of His care.

I lift my heart to the heights of God
Whose lips taste sweet the snows,
Their waters moving on to bless
As a heart that overflows.

I kneel in awe at the Mount of God
Where oak and cedar share
The loving touch of Eternal Hands.
I know that He is there.
- RSM

8

Above the distractions of the earth He sits enthroned;
All things are open to His divine survey;
And from His great and calm eternity
He orders that which His providence sees best.

—MH 417

CHAPTER 2

WHEN ALL ELSE FAILS, READ THE INSTRUCTIONS

Backdrop. *We will never forget the first time we visited Henry Martin's showroom in Grants Pass, Oregon. He had a fine assortment of automobile dealerships: Mercedes-Nissan-Volvo. Through the mail, we had ordered European delivery of a car in 1964, and had such satisfactory service that we were curious about this place and its people. Then we saw a plaque on his office wall: "When all else fails, read the Instructions." Just below and to the right was a picture of the Bible. It marked the godly boldness of a man who had been a prodigal in his early years.*

Henry uses his Bible as an experienced traveler treats a top quality map. God blesses the "almost magic" Weimar Institute diabetes and heart seminars he and Weimar physicians present across America and around the world. In a few days they deliver adult-onset diabetics from years of physical hell. And they give God all the credit through Ellen White [EGW].

Our Savior has given us His Word—an overall map that has all the basic information we need to experience his healing for eternity, and EGW's fine line map based on the big Map, so helpful for our time. But, like the patients of Henry's teams, they are healed as they obey diligently with love, and gratitude for God's specific directions through Ellen White for these unique endtimes.

In complex periods and times throughout history, God has raised up leaders—messengers or prophets such as Noah, Joseph, Moses, Isaiah, Jeremiah, Daniel and John the Beloved. Can you imagine that a consistent, all-wise, omnipotent God would leave us without a special messenger for endtimes in which He prophesies the worst trouble this world has ever known? Never! In Joel 2 He describes those times and foretells young men and women prophets He will send. Sure enough, there have never been such complex times that try men's souls as now, and He has sent a messenger!

Indeed, God's messenger, Ellen White, meets all the Bible criteria for a divinely-inspired prophet—as told in Isaiah 8:20 and 2 Chronicles 20:20. Her detailed commentary, counsel and warnings are Bible-based just as detailed local and regional maps from your automobile association or Rand-McNally are based on national or world maps. **If we study carefully, and avoid dangerous**

9

roads and take the safest, surest way Home. These directions are given in terms of the ethics, rapidity and languages of our times that are unique in history. We can get there with the Bible alone as our map or guide. Yet how thoughtful of God to provide additional directions appropriate to the atmosphere, subtleties and expressions of endtimes. Let's follow Him! William Andress treats *obedience* and our goal of eternal certainty with a poignant allegory that asks a big question: [*COLLEGIATE QUARTERLY*, **Last quarter, 1997, Adapted**] Jesus and Gabriel were taking a walk through an area of heaven reserved for the saints. Soon they reached a ridge that overlooked a gorgeous valley where animals frolicked on colorful carpets of fragrant flowers and grass, and birds filled the air with song.

Gabriel turned to the Savior and asked, "Master, this is one of the most beautiful spots in heaven." When are You going to bring the saints up to occupy it?" Deep in thought, the Savior made no reply but walked on to an even more glorious spot. Again Gabriel's inquiry went unanswered. At last they reached the New Jerusalem which reflected the Creator's radiance. Gabriel couldn't contain himself. "Master, nothing You have created is so dazzling. But the mansions are empty! When will you bring the saints?"

Then Gabriel noticed tears on the Master's face unlike any he'd seen since Jesus wept over Jerusalem 2000 years before. Wiping His tears, Jesus looked at Heaven's angel leader and asked, **"Gabriel, don't they want to come home? Don't they want to come home?"**

Martin and Andress beg questions that won't go away, and answers that Jesus needs: Why not read and obey the Instructions? How badly do we want to go home? Aren't we modern Israel who are honored with a modern prophet? Don't we have Truth to make us free? [Isa 30:21; Deut 28 KJV; RC 24]

Giving and carrying out precise instructions is a practice that is a bottom line in all sound vocational, professional or business transactions. How dependable are *our* maps, *our* instructions? How much do we know about them and what they have to offer? Are we aware of the eternal heavenly treasure that they chart in greater detail than any other, and how they guarantee a *life that measures with the life of God?*

What, for example, is unique about the details of our map? Does it cover health? education? lifestyle? Don't we have a totally Bible-based prophet, inspired by the Savior who died for us? Is there another church or people who can honestly make that claim? Our loving, inspiring Father, like any wise parent, means exactly what He says. He fused our modern prophet with Scripture which we call "The Spirit of Prophecy." And He awaits to empower our claim. Do we study enough to find Him?

It appears that some of us ministers--and perhaps laity--are not well-read on how God wants us to run His Church. Or of those who do read, some may not obey. We don't say this critically, but factually. Some years ago when the

Following are findings of an Andrews SDA Seminary study of ministers' reading habits that may offer one reason:

Title of Book	Have read		Have not read	
1. Acts of the Apostles	84	76%	15	15%
2. Adventist Home	76	69%	16	5%
3. SDA Commentary	27	25%	48	44%
4. Counsels on Diet & Foods	62	56%	45	41%
5. Child Guidance	35	36%	73	66%
6. Counsels on Health	33	30%	76	69%
7. Christ's Object Lessons	90	82%	20	18%
8. Counsels on Stewardship	31	28%	79	72%
9. Counsels to Parents, etc.	25	23%	84	77%
10. Desire of Ages	108	98%	2	2%
11. Education	80	73%	30	27%
12. Evangelism	74	67%	36	33%
13. Early Writings	81	74%	27	25%
14. Fundamentals of Christian Ed.	29	26%	81	74%
15. The Great Controversy	101	92%	6	5%
16. Gospel Workers	68	62%	42	38%
17. Life Sketches of EGW	70	64%	41	37%
18. Thoughts from Mount of...	89	81%	21	19%
19. Ministry of Healing	87	79%	24	22%
20. Medical Ministry	18	16%	92	84%
21. Messages to Young People	69	63%	41	37%
22. Prophets and Kings	86	78%	24	22%
23. Steps to Christ	101	96%	3	3 %
24. The Sanctified Life	60	55%	50	45%
25. Selected Messages, I & II	47	43%	63	57%
26. Story of Redemption	57	52%	53	48%
27. Testimonies, 9 Volumes	37	34%	73	66%
28. Testimonies to Ministers	57	52%	53	48%

Note the percentages of the operations or methods books such as:

Testimonies, 9 volumes	34%
Child Guidance	36%
Counsels on Health	30%
Counsels on Stewardship	28%
Fundamentals of Christian Education	26%
Counsels To Parents, Teachers & Students	23%
Medical Ministry	16%

media was full of news about rampant disease from beef, chicken and fish, Worthington Foods asked us to do a study, using a national sampling in which we found that about half of our American Adventists in the East and West eat meat regularly, with the percentage in the Midwest running around 52%. I got to thinking: Why does industry pay dearly for a top consulting engineer? Why does God give us inspired authority?

One time I shared a podium with a chap by the name of Peter Drucker at a Columbia University retreat. I wasn't impressed with the man...until he opened his mouth. Soon I knew why he was preeminent and on boards of great corporations. Then I thought, How about God? If I have my act together, won't I revere Him even more, and do what He directs to the best of my ability? Do I listen when He opens His Mouth, an Infinite Counselor who is on call every moment of every day? Is there any job more important than running God's institutions or industries, or guiding His people? Why do we hear derision about reforms in health, education, stewardship, etc. when our friends are following something as simple as 1 Corinthians 3:16, 6:19 and 20, and 10:31?

Except for a few of the standard inspirational volumes like Steps To Christ, Desire of Ages, Evangelism, Great Controversy, Ministry of Healing, and *Education* (which many have read during college days), the Seminary Study Report suggests that we are fortunate if we have a pastor who knows God's modern prophet well. How about the rest of us? Do we have any less accountability? I can hear Enoch, Elijah and Moses welcoming Ellen White to the inspirer's club.

Even more crucial, the most neglected of her books are what might be called *operational,* that tell us how to *operate* the Church and its institutions. Only a third or less of the pastors and pastors in training in the study had read such books as *Counsels on Health, Counsels on Diet and Foods, Medical Ministry, Counsels to Parents, Teachers and Students, Fundamentals of Christian Education,* and the *Testimonies* (nine volumes). Yet these are our main sources on the principles and methods which identify long-time godly institutions. Consider the Tokyo and Manila Sanitariums and Hospitals and national records for their top nursing schools or long-time work-study schools like Tennessee's Laurelbrook or Little Creek, and Weimar Institute's *pioneering NEWSTART: Nutrition, Exercise, Water, Sunshine, Temperance, Air, Rest and Trust in God,* imitated by many and rated as one of America's top three lifestyle centers.

Add to this shortfall such instruction as *Counsels on Stewardship* offers on wills and legacies in which we are instructed to give our fortunes to the gospel work instead of to children who aren't in need. And consider well-reasoned directions on medical institutional salaries in *Medical Ministry,* and on locating hospitals in *Counsels on Health.*

12

Read carefully the Scriptural and EGW quotations in the Box in the *Prologue*. Have we as church board members, pastors or parents worked to insure that our school or schools are prospering because they are committed to the Scripture and Spirit of Prophecy? Page 290 of *Patriarchs and Prophets* firmly states that our obedience to these counsels is a condition of our entrance to the Heavenly Canaan.

Nearly all of our serious institutional problems reflect apathy to, or rejection of, God's inspired EGW principles and methods. God says, "Prove me!" How do we really know Him if we have not experimented with Him? We can say this with certainty, although we have made mistakes running ahead of God. But we have tested this melding of obedience and prayer, and learned how the best of scientific research has embraced EGW in such areas as health, family, stewardship, institutional accreditation, et al—so wonderfully filled with miracles. We will tell you about them. It's exciting to test His instructions! Every true experiment returns a miracle! And what a challenge to assuage Jesus' tears. Yet tears or no tears, God holds us to strict account if we ignore the up-to-date maps to His city, based on His master map, the Bible. [CT102,94; EZE 18,33;DA 441] Let's look at many instances in the chapters ahead.

First, remember how disasters have come and gone throughout the ages with Israel and others from neglect, disobedience or rejection to God's prophets. Then compare it with today. Yet a recount of His blessings is far beyond human capacity to fully grasp. They are true miracles, replete with truth which glorifies God. Consider in the next chapter a few blessings...and very few curses in our church history.

"The very last deception of Satan will be to make of none effect the testimony of the Spirit of God," the instructions that make us unique. [2SM78] Adds Ellen White in ominous counsel, "I saw the principal and the teachers as they that must give account." To sit silently by with less than a thorough acquaintance with the Spirit of Prophecy, while boards, laymen, teachers and pastors permit or pursue conventional wisdom and practices, is to play eternal games with those in our care and give the back of our hand to God. [EZE 3, 33] One day outside the City, if we read this clearly, they may cry bitterly, "We wanted to go home! Why didn't you lead us on the path to the City?"

We have nothing to fear for the future,
except as we...forget the way the Lord
has led us...in our past history.

—Life Sketches 196

CHAPTER 3

HOW THE CHURCH ITSELF
EXPERIMENTS WITH ELLEN WHITE

Backdrop. *We know that none of us is perfect except through the grace of Jesus. Yet to be balanced and fair, we will touch on both blessings and curses, personally and corporately, and conclude with blessings. We had the privilege of sharing several poignant, even exciting, eras of institutional development in the Church since 1933 when I first taught at Pacific Union College, and in 1935 when Dorothy first taught there. Even better were the honors of being mentored by men and women whom Ellen White [EGW] had personally led closer to God. Long before we were married, it seems that God had something in mind for us individually, although we had no idea of what He had in mind corporately. We first give you a cheering picture of the General Conference and our prophet early in this book.*

General Conference. At the outset we must be clear on one matter: When one is viewed as a reformer (although we have never rejoiced in the overtones of that word) some people assume that he is critical of leaders in high places. Not necessarily so. He knows he needs them all the more. Most of the key leaders that we know have been deeply consecrated. If we have questions, and if it is any of our business, we go personally to them. They have usually been voices of God on earth to us, often maligned, but seldom guilty. All, as we recall, have deeply respected Ellen White. When they do overlook or reject her God-given counsel, they, like the rest of us, regret their actions.

Presidential mistake. One of the most moving was General Conference President A.G. Daniels who ignored Ellen White's words against flesh foods [*The Later Elmshaven Years* 198-207; CDF 380]. He heard her, yet apparently didn't realize that God had firm reasons for telling her that translated saints would eat like heaven—without flesh foods—which will certainly ease the transition to a place where there will be no flesh foods. Attending doctors told how Elder Daniels, once stubborn, finally and fully obeyed God through Sister Ellen's instructions as he lay dying of abdominal cancer. There he said, "Don't pray for my healing....Pray for my salvation."

Presidentially correct. In a widely-discussed court case, a General Conference president was blamed and harassed for years for remarks that reflected harshly on the Roman Catholic Church, contrary to Mrs. White's

14

counsel. I knew him well, and couldn't believe the vicious rumors, so I asked him. The facts, never generally known, showed that a non-Adventist attorney retained by GC officials had made the comments, thinking that Churchmen would like such blunt remarks. Yet they were laid on the shoulders of a Godly GC president, who after a long delay was exonerated, although the rumor mongers trail will not likely be erased on this earth.

Another wide-ranging matter concerned *Medical Ministry,* an EGW operational book which, as we have noted in part, is replete with detailed guidelines on institutional size, staffing and wage scales but has been read by relatively few ministers. During a period when GC actions were taken that did not support her God-given counsel against high salaries for medical administrators, the same president was roundly criticized. We also seriously doubted these charges. When we checked, we found that the president had tried firmly to persuade divisional and union conference and institutional leaders to obey God's counsel through Mrs. White against high salaries.

The EGW message was reasonable and logical in terms of the Church goals. God had discouraged bigness and high salaries: Institutions were to be limited to sizes that could be staffed entirely by godly members of the Church. Salaries were to be modest, with minimal disparity between employee levels. Ministerial salaries were one measure, but allowed for costs of professional specialization. In answer to those who insisted that high salaries were necessary to secure qualified managers, EGW had made clear that God would provide highly-qualified godly employees. All who know the story of Elijah and the 7000 saints God had in reserve, know that He always has willing and qualified personnel waiting for positions He approves for institutions He sanctions. Rejection of this counsel has caused no end of doubt and distress, so *some key hospital employees refuse high salaries. Those who do not may be at risk.* [Deut. 28:15-68]

Ellen White has made the same principles and methods clear in developing, staffing or locating health and educational institutions at all levels. Here are several examples:

Andrews University and the U.S. Commissioner of Higher Education. Sometimes men of other faiths embrace our instructions more carefully than we. During Potomac University's (now Andrews) earliest years, Dr. Lloyd Blauch, U.S. Commissioner of Higher Education, chided us gently when he learned that the name of our university was *Potomac.* "Did you know," he asked, "that was the name of a diploma mill?" That shock set off a hurried search by the University Board for a new name.

But before long, word was passed that several of our faculty who had overlooked EGW counsel to locate out of the city, were buying homes near our University headquarters at the General Conference on the northern border of Washington, D.C. They were urging relocation of our fast-growing institution on two or three acres between Takoma Academy and a nearby gulch. Again Dr. Blauch made a comment: "I thought you were *country* people." Then he added "Stay on target. Follow your lady!" When Elder Paul Bradley, then GC Associate Secretary insisted that I present this to the GC Autumn Council, there was again an immediate, almost frantic, reaction by the concerned faculty members. After a few carefully-controlled, though warm exchanges, the Council took Dr. Blauch's and "our lady's" (EGW's) advice and began looking for a property in the country. After failure to reach early agreement on properties near the District of Columbia, the Board accepted an offer from Lake Union Conference President Jerry Smith and Emmanuel Missionary College President Floyd Rittenhouse for 40 campus acres in Berrien Springs as a gift, with the understanding that EMC would be the University undergraduate school. It subsequently was renamed "Andrews."

Voice of Prophecy and EGW. GC Vice-president Elder Willis Hackett, my board chairman when I was president of Philippine Union College, told me about his first meeting as a member of the VOP Board: Their non-Adventist radio agent hosted a steak dinner for the group. A firmly practicing vegetarian, Elder Hackett asked for a vegetable plate instead of eating around his steak. He was soon followed by most others. Conscience overruled convention and at future meetings vegetarian meals became the order of the day.

College of Medical Evangelists/Loma Linda University. When its Board reorganized CME as Loma Linda University, it first voted to go with God's instructions in *Counsels on Health* 166, *Evangelism 406* and *Medical Ministry* 305 and to build away from Los Angeles and the large cities in Southern California, and consolidate the clinical division of the Medical School with its pre-clinical division at Loma Linda, which was then a small town surrounded by orange groves and away from the cities. I was fortunate to be its corporate vice-president during this period. Yet at first the Board was under intense pressure from Los Angeles Campus physicians who served them, to reverse its action. So it voted to consolidate in the Los Angeles Campus area of Boyle Heights, a city ghetto so perilous that the nursing students had to be escorted from their dormitory to the hospital one block away. Humanly speaking, it was the expedient thing to do. And it should be noted at this point that these were conscientious men and women, as shortly will be seen.

I asked Chairman M.V. Campbell, a General Conference vice-president, if he thought God would bless with the funds we needed for a transition from CME to LLU if we disobeyed His orders and built in L.A. [Deuteronomy 28:1-14 KJV] He shook his head and replied, "No. In fact I just finished reading about that in *Medical Ministry.*" He had just studied this fine-line Map through Ellen White that is second only to the Master Map that is the Bible, and Elder Campbell now knew where to lead. Within a year the Board reversed itself again and voted to follow the directions of "One who presented this matter very

16

clearly" not to build in L.A., but to consolidate in Loma Linda. And that was another story.

Revered elders and physicians like Elder Glen Calkins, retired vice president of the General Conference and a former leading Southern California businessman, Elder C.L. Bauer, retired president of the Pacific Union Conference and former vice-chairman of the Board, and Dr. Steen, actively led a team of physicians and others such as Doctors Marion Barnard, Bernard Briggs and Mervyn Hardinge, and laymen such as Clyde Harris, *who had read the Instructions* and determined to obey them. When they heard of the decision for Los Angeles, they prepared a letter to present to the General Conference Session at San Francisco, and rallied a reported 1500 alumni to back Loma Linda as the locale for the University Medical School. When GC President R.R. Figuhr heard of this, he ordered Editor Francis Nichol to stop the *Review* presses, and hastily wrote an answer from information supplied by Los Angeles proponents, not realizing that some salient facts were missing. The Bauer-Calkins-Steen team took care to counsel with others, including Drs. Hardinge and Briggs, and wisely decided to wait until after the San Francisco meetings for their second letter. When they did, the Board, influenced by Clyde Harris, President C. A. Scriven of the North Pacific Union Conference and others, voted finally for Loma Linda. **[See the Appendix at the end of this book for the Bauer-Calkins-Steen story. This account was verified among others by Drs. Briggs and Hardinge above, by GC officers Neal Wilson and W. J. Hackett, and by Charles Hirsch, then GC educational director, four of whom are still living at this writing in Spring 2001.]**

God promised through *Deuteronomy 28* and *Education 50* that prosperity will "overtake" us when we obey "diligently." Sure enough, after the Board's 1962 vote to obey God's EGW counsel, a LLU fund-raiser later reported more gifts in three years than in the previous 40 years.

Devotion to conventional wisdom and educational patterns of the world often balks at any tendency to take our prophet seriously. Some say she is not our Bible, but only an inspired commentator. The first is true. The second is not. The people who doubt have not thoroughly experimented with her, and in this respect, with God. She was God's *messenger*, inspired by the same Holy Spirit as Isaiah and Jeremiah, and fits Biblical criteria for latter-day prophets. [Joel 2:28; 2 Chron. 20:20; Isa. 8:20] In our seminars those of other faiths eagerly buy her books, impressed by her godly counsel on education, and testimony from science and secular authorities. Thousands from other faiths embrace her message. See Chapters 15 and 16 for some examples.

Others say that EGW instructions are out of date, or are for another time, or were planned only for a certain level of schools. They don't reckon with the certainty that her Author is God and He speaks to all levels. Note the precision and coverage of His Instructions—from all grade levels to junior college in the

San Fernando School in *Counsels to Parents, Teachers and Students 211,* and *Fundamentals of Christian Education 41*, through to LLU in *Medical Ministry* [MM] page *81*. And it is for our times. [ED 50. Also PP 290, ED 210, 226, FE 512, CT 211, FE 41] Yet the key operational books *Medical Ministry, Fundamentals of Christian Education* and *Counsels to Teachers* are among her least read. *Let's remember that the Holy Spirit audits our institutional practices according to God's Counsel, blessing when we obey, cursing when we don't.* [Deut 28]

Master counselor. Our modern prophet is broad and deep. She accurately foresaw the San Francisco Earthquake. She predicts New York skyscrapers burning as if made of pitch. [LS411, 9T94-95, 13] Her books are much more than a hoard of essays on adornment and diet and dress. She wrote on marriage relations, business management practices, family life and birth control. When Mrs. White learned that a certain man reserved intimacy with his wife only for conception of children, Elder Loughborough quoted her as telling the chap, "Go home and be a man!" [*Ministry*, April 1969, p23]

She even counsels on wills and institutional pay [see pages 323-335 of *Counsels on Stewardship*. See also 8T 216, 2SM 179-209]

God designs that teachers show by example—by working with students— how to build character and make a living. Parents and pastors are to work with them, too. The best youth camps use work with great success to develop manual skills and reverse negative values trends [FE 512, 41, CT 211, 283, Deut 28:13] See Chapter 10 that offers a brief test and thoroughly presents the blessings of a work-study-service balance, especially when shared by adults.

Should we expect the Latter Rain of the Holy Spirit when its influence is "counteracted" by amusements and sports? [FE220-30] What do we think God is thinking when a Conference flier for a "SPORTS LEAGUE" is slipped into each church's Sabbath bulletin, asking members to "submit" or "enter" a league team. Does He really mean what He says when He asks EGW to warn that He will hold principals and teachers "to account" if they refuse to follow His counsel. Let's look carefully at the "Directions" before we induce enrollments in our schools by touting intercollegiate team sports. There is more on this in Chapter 11.

The weaker and more helpless you know yourself to be,
the stronger will you become in His strength.
The heavier your burdens, the more blessed the rest...
—Ministry of Healing, 73

CHAPTER 4

GOD'S MIRACLE AT USC

Backdrop. *How does God show you that He really wants you in His work? Dorothy's folks were unfriendly at first to the idea, so we didn't think much about it. But God has ways of making Himself known. He had kept His hands over Dorothy and me for many years. He had healed me as a child from scarlet fever, the deadly influenza of World War I, and polio. Repeatedly He saved my life on the highway while driving truck and trailer for Dad. At least four times in the air His great Hand reached down over me and shielded me from certain death: on wartime inspection trips in New Guinea, and a disappointing delay of my flight home at War's end only to find that my scheduled flight had gone down in the Pacific Ocean between Honolulu and San Francisco. He turned away adders in the New Guinea jungles, and the slopes of Turkey's Mount Ararat. Some say "mere coincidence" or "a matter of timing." What did God have in mind? Time after time, Dorothy and I needed evidence that no man could gainsay...and we got it, most unexpectedly.*

After World War II as a California city school superintendent, we retained University of Southern California **[USC]** Dean-elect Irving Melbo as consultant for a school bond issue to build another school in our fast-growing system. The bond issue went well, yet Dorothy and I were startled when Dr. Melbo offered me a teaching fellowship at USC. I had no ambitions for anything higher than a master's degree, and appropriate credentials as a good school administrator, which were largely in hand.

Yet, *after* we signed on, he urged me to do doctoral study, offering free tuition as a staff member. Although I had no confidence in myself as a scholar, we did have four years of unused World War II U.S. GI-Bill money for education and family support, and Dorothy had saved frugally the nearly two years I was in wartime New Guinea and Philippines. She had also built us a nice little house while I was overseas. We hoped to finish the degree within USC's normal 4-year minimum.

Once a Methodist Seminary, USC was variously called the "Columbia or Harvard of the West." It was also the *alma mater* of Dr. Charles Weniger, my major professor at PUC 10 years before. But since USC was rugged in my fields of child development and teacher education, I could take even longer, especially since I was teaching half time.

Into this fantasy intervened grey-headed churchmen who warned that if we studied in this "worldly" environment, we would surely lose our walk with God. Dorothy and I knew only too well of classmates who had lost their way, so we took their counsel seriously. Later this seemed really ominous when a former Adventist professor at a leading Adventist college was assigned to my doctoral committee—the only one who gave me trouble about Sabbath classes. So we followed Paul's counsel to the Philippians [2:10,11], knelt, and confessing the Name of Jesus, we told our Heavenly Father that we claimed His Psalm 91 promises: We would dwell in the secret place with Him, in the certainty that He would cover us with His wings.

We decided that I would take no home-work home. We would put Dennis, then 21 months old, to bed, and settle down for a couple of hours with our Bibles and Ellen White books whose value by now had become very real to us. That turned out to be one of the most rewarding decisions we ever made. The information and inspiration God endowed during those hours empowered a timeless chain of EGW-related miracles. With only 10 classes to teach weekly, I could spend the remainder of each day on a doctoral program.

Each evening we studied and prayed for two hours or so until we read the Bible and nearly all the EGW books, which clearly proved to us that she was God-inspired. Early each morning at 6:30, after family worship and breakfast, I drove a car pool to the USC Campus before heavy traffic, in time to find a parking place. In June, 1946 I settled into a neat little pad on the Doheny Library's third floor directly above its main entrance.

As I focused on two areas, child development and learning, and on reorganizing and accrediting universities and colleges in teacher education, God clearly had His own timing: He went before me, providing grace with my professors, arranging things about which I was not bright enough to ask. His Hand was in every academic and personal transaction, meshing schedules, voluntarily reducing my Ed.D. credit demands 12 hours to the requirements for a Ph.D., even coordinating dissertation and examination schedules. Yet we were astounded when in April 1947 Dr. Melbo told me that my final oral exam and graduation was scheduled for May 1947, three years early!

Another amazement waited in the wings. Because of my phenomenally brief doctoral period, the dean's big office was filled with curious guests, most of them doctoral colleagues. Staffers told me the psychologists and philosophers would make it a field day, striking at each other by bouncing questions off of me. I had prayed for clarity of mind and didn't feel too stressed; Dr. Melbo had said, "You know a lot more about your topic than anyone else." That initiative is one purpose of doctoral research. But that day God gave me words that were not my own. The really tough questions were not about my dissertation.

20

The first fifteen or twenty minutes went quickly, and all seemed satisfied with my study. Then they turned to more cunning questions. For example, preeminent philosophy professor Merritt Thompson asked, "What is your definition of an authority?" Any scholar should know that answer, for the whole USC doctoral program was designed to build highest standards for *truth*. But the question became ominous, for I had authorities all around that big table. And I had an obligation to the doctoral candidates listening closely along every wall.

When I hesitated momentarily, Dr. Thompson, in his typical dry humor put me explicitly on the spot: "Do you consider Dr. (D. Welty) Lefever an authority?" Of course he was; he was also preeminent, a principal child guidance author for New York's Ronald Press. Yet for a moment I was confused. In that room, before that crowd, would it be good judgment to say, "Yes?" Would I be selling my soul as a flatterer? I am certain that in that split second God's Holy Spirit took control. He knew D. Welty Lefever and his happy disposition.

I answered, "No, sir."

In a sense I was saying that Dr. Lefever was quite ordinary, when everybody knew he was a world leader in guidance, and was one of my most loved and respected professors.

There was a stunned silence at the table and among the emerging scholars around them. They later confided that the thought flashed among them, "Doesn't Ray Moore know Welty Lefever? Is he really saying that the world-known guidance author is not an authority?" Momentarily, as it were in the final act of an exciting play, Dr. Lefever turned on his famous grin, leaned back in his armchair, and glancing around the room, nodded and led the crowd in roaring applause.

Only then did I really grasp what would have happened if I had expediently answered, "Yes." What my answer did say to the committee is, "Moore must have a very high standard for an authority." But these were God's words; I was not that bold nor bright. The chairman pounded his gavel and dismissed me for the committee vote. Minutes later he called me back and with a big smile said, "Congratulations! Session adjourned." My "two-hour" final examination was over in 30 minutes. *God had done it again.* He had blessed those nights with Dorothy, Scripture and Ellen White in place of homework. We were walking hand-in-hand with the Holy Spirit who had inspired God's prophet, EGW.

In 1947 without our initiative, the job offers started coming: one to direct student teaching at Syracuse University, whose dean, Maurice Troyer, was one of my USC summer professors. Another to be curriculum director at the College of Medical Evangelists (now Loma Linda University); still another to be dean of Philippine Union College which was scheduled for upgrading. And one to head education and psychology at La Sierra College as a full professor. But the last, and for the time being, the least, came from Pacific Union College. Did God have a plan for us! He was in His heaven, and all would be right with our world.

Many, including some relatives, thought we were "just lucky." Yet we were now certain that for a Christian there is no such thing as luck. To admit to chance is a slap in the Face of God, when we are under His care. He was always there. We often agreed that we needed more bending of knees. His assurance has always been beyond our efforts to selflessly respond to Him as Abba Father--*our own* Father—in boldness making claims on Him. [Rom 8:15]

PUC meant a lot to us as our *alma mater,* yet at first it seemed to have the least to offer. However it had a great inner appeal. We decided to seek counsel from the man I would be following. This meant that I would be taking the baton from the eminent Guy Wolfkill, a University of California-Berkeley genius who had been my major professor in the 1930's, and upon whom many students looked with awe, I among them. He was a man of masterful integrity, and of terrifying temper when he observed a clear violation of the college's impeccable standards. He had retired, but would stay on or near campus. An inner voice seemed to be moving us toward PUC; yet I asked Dr. Wolfkill what he thought about my taking over his job in view of higher rank and pay offered by others; and who was I to replace him? He immediately insisted that *with Dorothy*, we were "ideal" replacements. His shoes were way too large for me to fill, yet we knew that God could make up the difference.

In these frankly scary times, we often reel in wonderment at the reality and assurance of being moment by moment under the wings of a personal God who gave His Son for us at the risk of His eternal loss. He was even patient during uncertainties that intruded during the times we ran ahead of Him or when I allowed "urgencies" and "emergencies" to preempt Him.

Eventually we came to the practice of talking with God not only daily, but moment by moment. Every decision of our lives–even minor ones—had to be His—every thought, word and action. That was a heavy assignment, so Dorothy and I asked Him to help us approach Him more and more intrepidly, and always with specific thanksgiving, in things little and big. *Until then, most of my testing had been private, confidential—protecting my ego in case He didn't answer my prayers as expected. [Heb4:16] I had really worried about "going public" in prayer. [Isa26:3; Jer29:13]* He settled that. During the next five years we had a train of experiences with Him, the first of hundreds in our last 50 years as we became more daring in testing Him. Not perfect, but certain that He liked to be tested, and making us more thoughtful when we put Him to a test, to give God a chance to prove Himself.

Then came a crisis call we had to know for sure if it was from God. EGW's chapter on "The Privilege of Prayer" (the name of that section in most editions) in *Steps to Christ* meant a lot to us. More about that kind of praying in Chapter 6, "When is a call from God?" Meanwhile, in the offing, we had a test at Pacific Union College, a test of and for the whole college.

Lean not unto thine own understanding.
In all thy ways acknowledge him,
And he shall direct thy paths.

—Prov. 3:5,6

CHAPTER 5

GOD'S KIND OF ACCREDITATION

Backdrop. *The next month after my doctoral final in late May, 1947 we joined the Pacific Union College [PUC] faculty where President Percy Christian soon asked me to head the Masters program in teacher education, the area of my doctoral major. It was clear that God preferred PUC as our first post-doctoral assignment over what appeared to be rosier posts in other Adventist institutions or as director of student teaching at Syracuse University. PUC was a small but highly-rated school near the head of California's pastoral Napa Valley where I had worked my way in the middle of the Great Depression between 1932 and 1938. Although the College Board asked me also to head the Division of Psychology and Education, my faculty rank was assistant professor, the least of our job offers. Maybe God was testing us. But that was quickly rectified without any protest from us. We had asked God's direction. He was testing us. Before long, to our total surprise, He arranged a full professorship.*

Within a year or so, the Board asked us to try for PUC's accreditation for California State teacher certification and recognition of its masters degrees. Some colleagues thought the idea was preposterous. No American Adventist college had liberal arts accreditation at the master's degree level, although we were able concurrently to help Walla Walla College take the same track. Yet at the time, California was considered the most difficult state in the U.S.

By early 1949 we had organized a Teacher Education Council [TEC] and had worked out a sound plan for our accreditation attempt for State authority to recommend and expect approval for teaching licenses from Kindergarten through Junior College. Yet in the Church, men whom we deeply respected like Arthur Spaulding, GC President J.L. McElhany, *Review* Editor F.M. Wilcox, H.H. Votaw, and our dear friends E.A. Sutherland and P.T. Magan all cautioned about possibly violating a 1928 GC accreditation action. Some simply thought it nervy to expect any State favors. Yet as we read EGW carefully, we concluded that God encouraged professional licensing that would glorify Him. That was our implicit goal. So we moved ahead.

We soon realized that He had clearly set the stage. My study of teacher-education programs of California's 16 liberal arts colleges and universities was His idea, not mine. Before we left USC, we visited all of them and became familiar with their operations [Chapman, Claremont, Immaculate Heart, La Sierra, La Verne, Mount St. Marys, Occidental, Pepperdine, Whittier and University of Redlands in the South and Dominican of San Rafael, Holy Names, Immaculate Heart, Mills, College (now University) of the Pacific, San Francisco College for Women in the North and PUC].

But 1948-49 was a notoriously adverse time for schools seeking recognition for any kind of California State teaching licenses. Some institutions had been careless, and the State had become very strict. San Jose State University [SCSU], a major Silicon Valley school, had lost State accreditation for preparing teachers from junior high through junior college. Yet knowing we had a quality program, and were doing our best to meet God's conditions as a Christian institution, we decided to lay our faith on the line, and boldly claim His promises. Hadn't He insisted that if we diligently obey Him, His blessings will overtake us and make us the head and not the tail, above only and not beneath? [Deut 28:1,2,13 and Isa 54, 58, 60, and see page 2]

We reasoned that God likes to have His power challenged. If we had need and knew a billionaire board member who had written us to "Ask and ye shall receive" [John 16:24], and "Ye have not because ye ask not," we would be faithless and show disrespect if we asked him for only $15,000 when we needed $1,500,000. He would be honored if *for unselfish reasons* we asked for something only He could give us. Our TEC agreed, and we set out to test God.

In His Name we targeted our two most important and difficult teaching credential needs: General credentials in elementary and secondary education which in California licensed teachers from kindergarten through junior college, at the master's level. We also tried for specialist credentials in home economics, industrial arts and music. All operated on three levels: *Temporary* or probationary credentials for a year, *provisional* without inspection for a year, and *regular* with highest authority and no inspections for three years.

We made very clear in our thin proposal and the EGW book *Education* that our *philosophy calls for* a harmonious balance of mental, physical and spiritual powers. Our *goals* were godliness and sound American citizenship. Our *resources* included the Spirit of Prophecy and therefore the Holy Spirit, along with qualified personnel, funds and lovely mountain top facilities. And our *methods* to use those resources to reach those goals, based on that philosophy, were a balance of study, work and service—the teachers mentoring while working manually with the students. We told the inspecting team we were yet short on method. So the main part of our proposal was the book *Education*.

The chairman of our visiting evaluating commission was University of California-Berkeley's leading educational sociologist. Another was an equally distinguished Mother president of a leading Roman Catholic women's college. And yet another, was the president of Mills, one of America's ranking women's colleges. Some TEC members were surprised that the visitors did not judge

24

us by "worldly" standards. I learned of such integrity and openness for experimentation and creativity when evaluating some of the visitor's schools. As both institutional and federal education officer, I have found that this is a mark of most top evaluators. Besides, God had said, "If you do *My* will," didn't He? And didn't He promise "above all ye ask or think?" We were as sure that He was talking to us in His Word and through EGW as He had spoken to Israel through Moses at the Red Sea. [PP290] Yet we were especially on the spot before our faculty and Board.

All college department heads who composed the TEC joined loyally in preparing an utterly simple proposal. If we were to expect God's richest blessings, we must be brutally honest, cite our shortcomings as well as virtues and lay down our plans for correcting where we were short. From my experience with the California colleges and the State Board of Education and watching what they did to SJSU, all agreed: no hidden agenda. No pretense! No whitewashing so common to many such proposals, as I found years later when dozens of such documents came across my graduate programs desk at the U.S. Department of Education.

So instead of a typical, fat, expensively-bound proposal, we gave each visitor a lean document and a copy of the book *Education* by EGW, which was published in 1909 and best expressed our teacher education philosophy, goals, resources and methods. As the world's most widely published woman—by governments and sacred and secular publishers—EGW has been acclaimed by government officials and scholars around the world, as we shall note in Chapters 6, 15 and 16. We planned for "how and why" questions on every point—the kind of creative thinking to principle we expected of students—rather than to be mere reflectors of conventional wisdom and practice.

During the State Committee's visit, Chairman John Michaelis gave us very little inkling of his thoughts, yet we saw that the group liked the idea of training *teachers who would work manually with their students* in carrying out God's plan. They also liked our unique, but strict, screening of student teachers at a time when teacher education was in ill repute: We chose them early by giving them experience as teaching assistants as freshmen or sophomores instead of waiting until they had studied four or five years, and then we found they had little promise as teachers.

Yet the SJSU specter was always there. We hoped to receive approval for at least one credential. Then came the day when Dr.Michaelis and his committee met with us in President Christian's office. They seemed optimistic as they asked questions and made suggestions, yet didn't give any other clue as to their decision.

Only when I walked with Dr. Michaelis to his car, did I get a strong hint: He held up the red book *Education* we had handed to him along with our thin proposal. "Tell me, Ray," he asked, "where did you get this book?" He noted our 4-point harmonious balance of head, heart, hand and health that joined every teacher with students as mentors in study, work and service both in college classes and potentially in schools our students would teach as professionals.

I explained that we used it as a basic education philosophy textbook for *all* students. And how the homeschooled Mrs. White had only three grades of formal education, but was believed by many scholars, both religious and secular, to be a prophetess inspired by God. And many of the elements of our College's program were patterned after her interpretation of education in Ancient Israel and the life of the Christ child.

"I am not surprised," he rejoined, stroking the volume, "This book is 40 years ahead of mine that I just sent to press." Then he made a point which all Christian colleges would *do* well to follow, and which was confirmed when much later at the U.S. Department of Education where my job was to organize masters and doctoral program evaluations for approval of federal grants: They had it up to their gills with applicants who tried to impress more than to embrace principle. Dr. Michaelis was impressed with our candid proposal, *including our shortcomings*, and what we were doing about them. He was delighted that we never lost sight of our goals.

To see this done by a mature evaluator mix of secular, Protestant and Roman Catholic scholars was an education for our faculty. And six weeks later at a joyous, prayerful afterglow, with tears of relief and gratitude, we read the State's decision to the faculty and student body, and especially watched the faces of the doubters, who nevertheless rejoiced with us. PUC was approved at highest levels in all areas from Kindergarten through Junior College. All credit to God on His lady messenger.

There are some things
That we must understand to believe...
But the gospel
We must believe to truly understand.
-RSM

Before they call I will answer;
While they are yet speaking
I will hear.   —Isa. 65:24

CHAPTER 6

WHEN IS A CALL FROM GOD?

Backdrop. *In March of 1951, Dorothy and I were nestled with Dennis, then 5, and Kathleen, 2, on Howell Mountain above St. Helena on the eastern slopes of California's legendary Napa Valley, near the Pacific Union College campus. For nearly four years we had been tucked in a small, old two-story home cradled against the Cold Springs creek which in turn was laced with spreading California live oaks, as green the year around as the Ponderosa pines that tower over them.*

Decidedly primitive, without insulation, the cottage had one of those old-fashioned bathrooms whose tub rested on four "bear feet." Strung along our front yard were enough Gravenstein apple trees to yield yearly 200 quart jars of prime unsugared applesauce, many gallons of cider, and plenty of apples for our student and teacher friends who lived nearby. Dorothy and I couldn't be more blissfully settled than with our precious two bugs in this quaint Napa Valley "rug." Dorothy had recently declared that she must have powerful evidence "before ever moving from here."

Then a bright early spring day was clouded with a letter that threatened to turn our security into uncertainty, yet which some hailed as a flattering invitation—to head a college in Japan. Now we had to rethink Dorothy's ideas of "powerful evidence." Was the call really from God, as had been represented? It was especially distressing to Dorothy. She had found relief after nearly ten marriage years as a teacher and army wife who had born our children and shuffled from post to post with our two offspring, including my absence of two years overseas.

We weren't coveting a college presidency. Furthermore, this was a call to Post-War Japan and Okinawa. I had refused an army promotion offer if I would extend my overseas service to Japan as medical personnel officer on General Douglas MacArthur's staff in 1945. But that was to clean up after the war for the U.S. Army; *this* was to clean up for God's army, establish a Christian school system and upgrade a small college with endless problems: A 17,000,000 yen debt with no prospect of cash subsidy, no accreditation and low morale from post-War problems. Two academy principals had already refused the job.

Japan: God, the awesome logician. This was only two years after California State recognition of PUC's Masters Degree and teaching credentials. The General Conference was calling us to do an upgrading and accrediting job at Nihon Saniku Gakuin (Japan Three-fold School or Japan Junior College) that

27

was humanly impossible. Yet the binding goal of both the GC and the Japan Union Mission [JUM] was to produce mature ministers and credentialed teachers. The latter would require certification by Japan's Government under much more rigid demands than California's.

All was not doldrums. God didn't give us any rest, and we already knew that He delights to do what is humanly impossible. Deuteronomy 28 made it clear that we would never receive His blessing if we did not diligently obey His specific Instructions that He gave us through His prophet. Yet when we do obey Him, His Sky is the only limit. All would be up to Him, and He sees that we thrive on experimenting with Him.

The JUM problems did not stop there. The leaders said that we must take a car, for Japan manufactured no cars in 1951! All were imported. There was only one on the NSG campus. *And the Government demanded 100% of the vehicle cost for customs duties to import another.* Before we could give PUC notice, we must find if there was any way to avoid the tax. So Dorothy and I made that the main condition of accepting the call.

Meanwhile Dorothy's parents were bitter at the thought that we would minister to the country that had occupied their second-oldest son and their son-in-law for nearly five years in World War II. Nor had been the level of my love for Japan *as a nation* a credit to a Christian. Yet our first obligation was to God. And as if a portent of things to come, we had from 1947 to 1951 the help of excellent Japanese student secretaries, and in 1950 been rewarded with a 3-month teaching stint at PUC's college extension division in Hawaii. There the Japanese people, including college classmates, had adopted us. We learned to love them dearly as our own family, and still do to this day.

What did *God* want *us* to do? We heard how He had "called" people. Yet we were not conscious of the Heavenly Voice that Abraham and Moses heard. And we were cautious about using a fleece such as Gideon's, for ours was not a matter of life, death and national survival. How then do you know if a call is really from God?

It would be a decisive test. So we started on a frustrating merry-go-round search for information on tax exemptions: To the Japan Consulate in San Francisco who pointed to their Embassy in Washington, D.C. which in turn beckoned us to their Ministry of Finance (*Okurasho*) in Tokyo. Weeks turned into months of trying to contact Japan's various authorities, especially its financial arms. It became a yo-yo. We wrote to Okurasho. No reply. Then translated our inquiry into Japanese; no reply. Back to the Embassy which advised writing to the Japan's Bureau of Customs and Taxation. No reply. We wrote again in both English and Japanese with no reply. Was God testing us? Or were we testing Him? Our PUC colleagues said it didn't look as if God was calling us to Japan. It seemed that all our efforts had failed. When we were about to notify the GC that we were favoring PUC—God again showed His all-powerful Hand.

Our reasons for hesitating on the call were really selfish. Our only given *reason* was that we would have to take our own car. That would be $3000 taxes on our nearly new 1951 Ford, besides $500 to ship it—equivalent totally to more than $20,000 in present-day economy. But we did have the $3500, and knew that was a weak excuse.

April 15 had passed. PUC's employment deadline was only a month away. We had to give notice in a week or so, if we were to leave. We reminded God—as if we needed to—that time was wasting. He seemed so awfully slow. Yet I always regretted the times I ran ahead of Him. It's so easy to be humanistic—to follow our "wisdom" instead of walking with God where every breath is a prayer.

At the last minute one day, as a second thought, I invited Principal Willard Meier of the PUC Academy to go with me to a State teacher education meeting at Yosemite Park Lodge. He was a key member of our psychology and education faculty and might significantly benefit. And since I knew he liked to drive, two of us could go for the price of one. That invitation, although no genius of mine, turned out to be a great decision, for without a witness, the experience that followed would be unbelievable to many. As we drove down from PUC and the Silverado Trail of the pastoral Napa Valley to the winding Central California approach to Yosemite, Willard seemed possessed with the idea that we were more crucial to PUC than we would be at Japan.

"Besides," he insisted, "we all want you folks to stay here."

Finally I answered, "But the question is what does *God* want? How do you know when a call is from God?"

He agreed. In any event, we would soon find out. Willard would be available to give our PUC friends reasons if we did go, and excuses if we did not.

We turned into the Yosemite parking lot at nearly 8 p.m., shortly after sundown, and parked beside a Greyhound bus. Its last passengers—three distinguished-looking oriental men—had just retrieved their suitcases from the baggage compartment under the big gray vehicle. All were dressed in black suits, shoes, ties, flat-brimmed hats, and white shirts and were walking with their bags toward the registration office. They certainly didn't look like campers or vacationers. Nevertheless my heart jumped. Could they be from Japan? One looked to be about 45, and the other two in their mid 30's.

After we retrieved our bags and headed for the lobby to register, they were leaving. And again my heart jumped. What was this all about? Ten or fifteen minutes later, registered and settled, we went to the Yosemite Lodge Cafeteria for a light supper, and who should be sitting nearby at one of the big round tables but the three oriental men, strangely but obviously unhosted. My adrenalin was now pumping as we went through the food line. Was God about to give us an answer?

"Willard," I nodded toward the three men as we were placing our food on the table, "I need to talk with those men."

"Let's go," he agreed without hesitation.

So we left our food and quickly went over, bowing awkwardly. I'd heard they did that skillfully in Japan.

"Forgive me for intruding," I began, offering our names, "but are you possibly from Japan?"

All three stood quickly and bowed deeply. One of the younger men nodded, "Yes," and invited us to "Please sit down." He was the only one fluent in English.

"I am a college dean," I began and explained my question about our call to Japan, our plan to help a troubled college by showing teachers and students how to work and earn a living as well as to study from books. The teachers, we told them, did a much more effective job when working manually with them.

The men smiled and nodded.

Then we told them our need for a car, and that there might be exemptions from customs duties. We recited how we had contacted the San Francisco Consulate, the Embassy in Washington, D.C. and tried to contact the Ministry of Finance and Director of the Bureau of Customs and Taxation in Tokyo.

"Do you have *any* idea," I asked, "how we can know for sure?"

They talked briefly together, then the young man asked, "How long have you owned your car?"

"Since last September: Between six and seven months."

They talked together for a moment, then he smiled, "That is easy to answer. There will be no tax or duty on your car."

"We have heard that from several people," I replied slowly and apologetically, "I've heard all kinds of stories, but want to be absolutely sure. Where can I find out for sure? We have to face customs officers when we arrive at Yokohama."

He turned to the older man and spoke rapidly in Japanese, then looked to his other friend then back to us. "I can say positively that you will not have to pay any customs duty or excise tax if you take your own car to Japan."

Embarrassed that I had to be so insistent, but anxious to obtain some kind of documentation, I apologized profusely, then asked, "How can I secure some kind of document to show the customs officers at Yokohama? How can we be certain about this?"

With a word or two among themselves and understanding looks, each took his billfold from his pocket and handed me his card. They are on my desk here as I write. You will find them pictured on the next page.

Keiichiro Hirata, Director of Taxation and Custom Bureau, Ministry of Finance, Japanese Government. Keijiro Shoji, Tax Administration Agency, Ministry of Finance, Japanese Government. Mr. Kinnasuke Kishimoto, Tax Administration Agency, Japanese Government.

The men God used to direct us to Japan.

At the table before us sat the three men in the world, of all officials in Japan, who were the most qualified to answer my questions.

God had done it again.

We were sobered and excited, if that is possible all at one time. Surely the God of Heaven Himself had a plan for us. We would go! It was a very emotional moment for me, even brought tears—which doesn't happen often. Yes, we would go.

Then there were two sequels almost as exciting as the high point itself: We marveled how the Creator arranged all this.

First, the men had told us that they were there only over night and had to leave on the bus at 8 o'clock the next morning. Grateful to God and them, we offered to take them on a tour of the Park the next morning at seven, an hour before their bus left. That small courtesy apparently made a deep impression. Their delight was obvious, although we had no idea of what would come of all this when we arrived in Japan.

The next morning Mr. Kishimoto explained that they had been to an international monetary conference in Washington, D.C. They were scheduled to leave San Francisco for Tokyo on a Pan-American Airways Boeing Stratocruiser but "unaccountably" one its big port motors failed. This caused a 36-hour delay, just enough time, the San Francisco Consul told them, for the bus trip and 12 hours to rest. (And to meet with us and share Yosemite majesty).

The more we thought of it, the more we were in awe of the divinely-managed logistics: Along with all His other Universal business, God had looked ahead for months or a year or more in scheduling meetings, arranging unusual airline circumstances and a crucially pivotal meeting, with the best possible people, at precisely the right time to give us a simple and sure message. We have no idea how many factors God had to manage in order to work out our meeting, yet we found at least 10 complex elements:

1. The travels of three key Japanese officials who in turn had to clear with American and Japanese governments.

2. Dates of an international monetary conference for many nations in Washington, D.C.

3. An annual California Teacher Education Conference which had been arranged more than a year before.

4. A mission call from Japan which went through many hands.

5. The breakdown of a motor in a big plane in the right city.

6. The kind of mal-function that would compel a 36-hour delay.

7. An "impromptu" suggestion by the Consul General for the three to visit Yosemite—a most unlikely goal for these Japanese visitors, dressed as they were for Washington, D.C. business.

8. Our arrival at the precise moment as we parked, when the three men were the last to leave their Greyhound Bus.

32

9. Directing us to the parking place by the bus, and

10. Pointing us three times to the visitors before we were convicted enough to make a move. What a God!

Second, not long afterward, Mr. Hirata was named Vice Minister of Finance, the operating head of the Ministry. This meant that he had become Japan's most powerful non-political financial figure. And Kishimoto became head of a major corporation. God had left absolutely no doubts. *He was clearly expecting something special from us. This drove us to our knees, and still does,50 years later.*

Our arrival at Yokohama produced our third climax: When Dorothy, Dennis, Kathleen and I stepped off our ship, the *Philippine Transport,* and handed customs officials the three cards, their mouths dropped. They rushed us to their central office and scrambled to see who could do the most for us.

"God surely does things in style!" agreed our fellow workers. We cruised up the harbor road to Tokyo in our 1951 Ford, still lost in wonder at our royal welcome arranged by the King of kings who, *if we experiment with Him boldly,* leaves no doubt about His leading.

But that wasn't the end of Divine surprises! Our very low-paid Japanese staff inquired humbly if Mr. Hirata might possibly consider eliminating taxes on the tithe portion of their income, since the first 10% went directly to God to be used for the benefit of the Japanese. Mr. Hirata quickly agreed. This emboldened us to ask if we could also import and sell cars without import taxes--with all profits to pay our debts and aid our balanced work-study-service program--and how it would help Japanese youth. We would import cars with no taxation and sell them at market value which was more than twice what we paid. This along with unsolicited gifts, cleared the 17,000,000 yen debt we had inherited. We had *no* cash subsidy for the five years we were in Japan. All this from a meeting God arranged at Yosemite.

We also built and equipped five major college buildings, plus land and structures for a junior high school on an extended campus. For you who may wonder how we carried out Mr. Hirata's clearance, we imported Buicks, Chryslers and Mercedes, popular makes at the time in Japan—and on condition that we use our profits to build an institution that would improve Japanese education by using teachers to show students the value of manual work, how to earn a living, and in the process, to develop academic excellence, self worth, industry, creativity, strong character and sound relationships with God and man. Yet, we had forbidding obstacles! How could we become accredited?

If thou shalt hearken diligently unto to
voice of the Lord thy God, to observe and
to do all His commandments...The Lord
shall make thee the head, and not the tail...

--Deut. 28:1, 13

CHAPTER 7

ACCREDITATION OF GOD'S HIGHER EDUCATION

Backdrop. *In Japan, as in all of the universities or colleges whose management we have shared, we never negotiate on accreditation---not to be disagreeable nor confrontational, but to refuse compromise on principle. For example, we could not teach state-mandated courses that were not compatible with Christianity, including evolution, secular humanism, ad infinitum. We were turned down by the government, so we started making rounds of universities in search of affiliation. All were courteous, but none was interested in picking up a little school from the bottom of the academic ladder, in debt, and bound by unconventional religious beliefs. More demeaning were those who pitied us rather than simply telling us there was no chance. But we continued to pray, and this is God's love story:*

Tamagawa University was just about last on our Dean Toshio Yamagata's list of possible affiliation partners. It was an elite private school in Tokyo, known for its fine teacher education program. Our Japanese leaders deemed it beyond our grasp, yet in our extremity we must give God a chance.

Dr. Yamagata and our teacher-education head, Professor Funada, went to see the Tamagawa dean. Dr. Yamagata was stunned at first, but sure enough, it was Dr. Tsunekichi Mizuno, the head of social and religious education for Japan before and during World War II. In 1939, two years before the War, Yamagata and Francis Millard, our Mission and Board chairman, had asked Mizuno's permission to keep the little college open. Yamagata silently recalled how on that day in 1939 Dr. Mizuno listened with unusual concentration as he and Millard described their plans based on the Bible and the same book *Education* that University of California's Dr. Michaelis later praised at PUC and Dr. Florence Stratemeyer applauded at Columbia University. Dr. Mizuno was intent that day as they prayerfully, yet apprehensively, described their plans for Nihon San-Iku Gakuin [NSG], literally "Japan three-fold school," which stressed education for the head, heart and hand, and where students worked several hours daily with their hands. He waited until they "wound down."

"Is that all?" he asked.

"Well, yes..." was Yamagata's and Millard's apprehensive answer.

"Gentlemen," he said with great deliberation, his hands folded on his chest as he leaned back in his big chair, "I have read your book." Here he took a deep breath as if for emphasis, and spoke in excellent English. "I took it off the shelf in the University of Illinois Chicago Campus Library in 1926." He paused, his eyes closed, as if in deep reminiscence. "If you follow your plan," he said slowly and solemnly as Yamagata and Millard held their breath, "you have no reason to worry. If you don't follow your plan, you have no reason to exist!"

From that meeting, San-Iku Gakuin became the only foreign-origin school to remain open in Japan during the War. This same Tsunekichi Mizuno now was Tamagawa University's dean who quickly showed how favorably he remembered Toshio Yamagata and NSG.

"We will be glad to work with you," he promised Yamagata and Funada, "without the close institutional examination academicians usually expect under these circumstances."

"You understand that we are Christians?" Yamagata asked more in assumption than question. He was taking no chances, but remembered how during the War he had gone to prison for his faith, and some of his colleagues had died there. "We may have to ask for exceptions from time to time."

"I understand," assured the eminent and powerful dean whose word, unlike American universities, was law at Tamagawa. "There will of course be entrance examinations," Mizuno added. "But I am sure there will be no problem there."

Funada and Yamagata glanced at each other for a split second, and nodded. "*So desu-ne*," they agreed, but both of them later confided that this was stretching their faith, for they knew that Tamagawa normally accepted fewer than ten out of a hundred applicants. Both shuddered at what could happen if San-Iku students did not do well after all of Dr. Mizuno's kindness. But NSG now had a stronger work-study program than ever before, and we had every reason to make unusual claims upon God. Yet none of us was ready for the test God had in mind.

They returned to the campus with the great news, and we all thanked God. We canvassed the small student body for any who might be interested in being pioneers in this experiment. There were only twelve, and they were about as motley as Christ's disciples, except that there was no Judas among them. *All* were deep in prayer as they went to Tokyo, sixty miles away for the test.

All twelve failed.

When word reached us, we found as never before what it meant to "look through a glass darkly," as Paul describes the experience in 1 Corinthians 13. Our faith now was naked. Where had we failed? Or had we? What was God's design in this experiment which had gone so well this far? He knew our need for teachers. He knew our concern for His principles. Was there an Achan in our camp, someone somewhere who wasn't with us in full faith?

35

With such questions whirling in our minds, but with the promises of Deuteronomy 28:1-14 overriding them, Yamagata and Funada boarded the train again to Tokyo and Tamagawa. They would not go like puppies, with their tails between their legs, but would apologize frankly and without excuse and leave the matter in the hands of the distinguished deans and...in the Hands of God.

"I think I understand," Mizuno greeted them, even before they had a chance fully to extend their apology. "After all, your students are not trained in our philosophy. We will admit them on probation."

"All twelve?" Yamagata and Funada wondered, like two little boys in awe of a reprieve after being caught with dirty hands at the table.

"All twelve," the old dean assured them.

He quickly outlined the program: 1) The broad lesson outlines for the required courses—apart from Bible teaching—would be made by Tamagawa professors. 2) San-Iku professors would teach from the Tamagawa outlines. 3) The student papers would be submitted weekly to Tamagawa professors for grading, as were final examinations.

The only catch now was the fairness of the Tamagawa teachers, all of whom, we found, were bitterly opposed to arrangements made by their dean. The political science professor warned that the highest grade he would give under such circumstances would be a **B,** and there would be no more than one of them, if any at all.

This threat excited trepidation in the hearts of both our teachers, and students who came to Funada with the idea of dropping part of the work program in order to gain more study time. He came to Yamagata who came to me. The only question I could muster was, "God has brought us this far, what do *you* think? It was really more faith than I believed I had, but Yamagata was strong as usual.

"I am glad for your answer," he assured me. Then we prayed about it, and he went off to ask the same question of Funada who then passed it on to students and teachers. All agreed they would try God in this humanly-impossible test He had prepared for us. Yet they still were puzzled. Why He let them all fail the Tamagawa exam? We will tell you why in a moment.

No one can explain it, but it always seems to happen that way eventually when we set out to do exactly as God directs, and He starts blessing before we really get started. How? The students and teachers treated the hostile Tamagawa teachers with great respect, whether they deserved it or not. They did not let the pressures get them down. And the professors got the message. Before the end of the semester they made a group visit to the San-Iku campus at Naraha in Chiba Province, directly across the Bay from Tokyo. The students were at work, except for those that were on duty during other shifts.

"I can't understand," the visitors' leader commented, shaking his head, "how they do it, but they do. And a definitely superior job." The others nodded.

We would like to have told them that when you give all to God and experiment with Him, He somehow makes every act mesh with every other one, just as He had done during my doctoral year at USC. He provides creative thoughts so that you don't have to sit for hours turning a neat phrase or creating a worthy plan. These students were working hand in Hand with God who knew every thought in those professors minds and exactly how to please them in His way.

The proof lay not only in the change of the teachers minds, but also in the records they made that first semester: 106 **A**'s, 57 **B**'s and 6 **C**'s. Three and a half years later, ten of those twelve graduated with *shu* ratings, roughly the same as *summa cum laude* in America, or as Dr. Yamagata said simply, **"A- Plus averages."** The other two were slightly lower.

The students now knew why God had let them fail after preparing so hard for the entrance examinations. If they had all passed high at first, like kids on a water slide, the general impression would have been that they were highly-selected candidates. But we, and they, knew that they were a motley crew—all that San-Iku could scrape up as teacher candidates. All of us now knew that consummate failures had become the best single group in Tamagawa history. San-Iku Gakuin's credibility now rated with the best, and God was glorified. The more you try Him, the better equipped you are to experience the genuine excitement of waiting breathlessly through disappointment and even apparent failure to see how His omniscient Mind works in arranging complex circumstances to accommodate your godly needs. He is quick enough to share His infinite wisdom with you. One of these jewels was, "In patience, possess ye your souls."

This was a country in which it was so difficult at the time for a student to be accepted in a high school, that successful applicants in other schools grew long fingernails on their little fingers to show that they no longer could grab a hoe, no longer do manual work. Yet Scripture and EGW made it crystal clear that our prosperity was conditional on *diligent* obedience to God's plan. Otherwise we would rest under His curse. [Deut.28, ED50 and PP290] *And the same principles and methods apply today around the world.*

Soon our leaders in the field developed balanced programs in such schools as Kobe and Hiroshima. Dr. Yamagata verifies this as we write. Those academies still do today.

We are asked, "Exactly how did you ever start this?" When we determined to follow diligently God's balanced work-study-service education plan with all teachers joining students in manual work, we laid our hands on His Deuteronomy 28 vow that if we diligently obey, His blessings would *overtake* us and make us the head and not the tail, above only and not beneath. Yet we must admit that our hearts were in our throats the day our men visited Tamagawa University, the last school on our hopeful affiliation list.

37

All these blessings are documented: God not only opened the way to pay the 17,000,000 yen college debt without even a yen of cash subsidy from the Mission, He provided for extensive upgrading and renovation. He built and furnished buildings for administration, library, music, men's dormitory and a health-food industry which at our recent visit was reported to be the largest in the Division. He gave us the highest health rating of all Japanese universities, enabled our farm to be judged finest in the Nation, and gave us a problem we never could solve: He raised our enrollment from 128 to 450 so that we could accept only one out of every six applicants. And we were in tears of gratitude when our Board Chairman and Union president Elder Francis Millard told the students that our college and academy was winning more souls than all churches in Japan and Okinawa together—under leadership of Elders Thomas Blincoe, Sakae Fuchita, Shinsei Hokama, Shirou Kunihira and Dean Toshio Yamagata, and all the faculty and 98% of the student body.

On second thought, that was exactly what God had promised in Deuteronomy 28 and in Isaiah 54, 58 and 60. He had made us "the head and not the tail, above only and not beneath," and helped us "enlarge" and "lengthen our cords and strengthen our stakes," and to "Arise, shine" and "cry aloud."

As promised in Isaiah 58, He even had the Emperor's brother, Senior Prince Takamatsu, with his lovely princess, make one of the most winsome, wise and truly reverent tributes ever made about God's wisdom through EGW. Today it is a foreword in the Japanese edition of the EGW book *Education* in commemoration of NSG's inauguration as a senior college on May 6, 1952. You will find more in our Chapter 13 on honoring God.

> *Men travel from afar*
> *To climb the mountain tops,*
> *Yet they are content to tread only*
> *The foothills of their own souls.*
>
> -Anon.

Jesus said, "Suffer little children,
And forbid them not, to come unto me"
... And He laid His hands on them
—Matt. 19:14,15

CHAPTER 8

WHEN DELAY IS NOT PROCRASTINATION

Backdrop. *In Acres of Diamonds, Russell Conwell's famed Chautauqua story, Al Hafed hastily sold his large farm on the Indus River without checking well-researched geological maps, to fund a quest for fabled diamond sands. He searched haplessly along ocean shores until he was penniless, then drowned in a heavy surf. He never knew that a meticulous explorer who had thoroughly researched all likely resources had discovered a vast diamond deposit in the river sands snaking through his own backyard, now famed over the world as the Golconda Diamond Mines. America's quest for excellence—for healthy, creative, self-directed, student minds—could for the lack of attention to sound research and the writings of Ellen White, be headed for Al Hafed's fate.*

From Capitol Hill and the White House to the local school and the humblest home, Americans grope for answers to disastrous declines in literacy, skills, and moral behavior which threaten national collapse that may potentially outdo the downfall of Ancient Greece and Rome. Those who are elected to bar such a catastrophe do not appear to have the wisdom, moral courage and statesmanship of a Caesar Augustus and his Julian Laws that vetoed abortion and penalized young marrieds who didn't care for their parents. They spurn a close relationship between these problems the lifestyles that we impose on our children daily.

We parents, schoolmen, educational associations and legislators are responsible for pervasive child abuse: There is an absurd indifference to peer dependency that takes a child by any decent family by institutionalizing him with peers that form character more convincingly than adults. This rampant mental health nemesis begins in daycare and preschools.

Instead of studying how best to meet their needs, we reject research, idolize convention and put our "little ones" out of home, away from chores and values that produce outgoing, healthy, happy, creative children. In a federally-sponsored multi-university analysis of thousands of early childhood studies we carried out at Andrews, Loma Linda, Stanford, University of Colorado Medical School and the National Center for Educational Statistics, Moore Foundation researchers concluded that the United States rushes its little ones out of home and into institutional life years before most, especially boys, are ready.[1] The effect on their mental and emotional health is an inexcusable lifestyle perversion that destroys creativity and fosters illiteracy. Kids burn out and dropout rates skyrocket in mute testimony, although in some cases they, like Thomas Edison, are more fortunate than those who stay.

From Tufts' Piagetian specialist David Elkind to Cal-Berkeley's William Rohwer, dozens of child learning and development leaders warn that early formal instruction is burning out our children. Yet lawmakers in every American state, Canadian province and industrial nation, egged on by vested educators, ignore the research as if treating a common itch instead of a social cancer.

Since 1976, the National Education Association **[NEA]** leaders have been goading members, school boards and state legislators to lowering school entrance age to 3 or 4. The White House, governor's mansions, Congress and state legislatures mouth the crucial import of the family and children, yet turn their heads and raise their hands to vote money to encourage and accommodate parental dereliction and abusive action that shoves kids out of their homes long before they are ready, possibly unaware that they are creating failure, frustration, amorality and crime.

Don't count on this educational behemoth making sound educational sense. For example, NEA lieutenants like Senator Koch of Nebraska's legislature, frankly admitted years ago that they want little tykes in school by at least age 3 or 4 to develop a reservoir of teacher jobs. They give no serious thought to child welfare. They flaunt history, research and common sense and essentially say, "Nevermind children and families; we want dollars and jobs." Nor does this jell with the self-defeating NEA position on abortion which alone shorts the NEA an estimated 1,500,000 children annually.

Parents and teachers who try to cope with youngsters who are institutionalized early are also burning out. The learning tools of the average child who enrolls today between ages four and six or seven are neither tempered nor sharp enough for the ever-higher academic tasks laid on them. Worse still, we destroy our children's natural potential for creativity and altruistic sociability.

Consider the disastrous sequence we set off in a satanic mental and physical health cycle: 1) *fears*, as children, especially boys, are jostled out of family nests early into environments which limit or destroy values, 2) *dismay* at strait jacket social pressures, academic litter and behavioral restrictions in classrooms, 3) *futility* because unready learning tools—senses, reason, brain immaturity, coordination—cannot reach the mental rungs which formal lessons foist on tender nerves and minds, 4) *hyperactivity* growing out of nerves and jitter from such frustration, 5) *failure* which quite naturally flows from the four experiences above, 6) *delinquency* that for similar reasons is failure's twin, 7) a frequent, forced surrender to *peer-pressure, alcohol, drugs, illicit sex, violence and suicide.* 8) loss of altruistic social relations appropriate to their ages, attachment to gangs (After all, kids must have family) 9) early pregnancies and related burdens, 10) in turn generating unfit parents who produce more unfit kids for too-early school.

Indifference to the mental and emotional health of children is not new. The pages of history are replete with accounts of virile cycles which in every known case ended catastrophically. They usually began with vigorous cultures awake to the needs of children, and ended in the death of societies and empires as they surrendered family values and bonds.

Sound, replicable research and research analyses provide a precise link from past to present and affords a moving perspective on children today. Persuasive reasons exist for declining literacy, academic failures, rampant peer dependency and delinquency. All four act in concert to deny our goal of happy, confident children who are healthy in body, mind, and spirit. Whether or not we can be conclusive about causes, America's decline in literacy from the estimated over 90% in the 19th and 20th centuries to its 50% functional literacy today parallels the parental scramble to institutionalize children at ever younger ages.[2]

Harvard's Carle Zimmerman and Frances Frederick La Play found that America echoes Ancient Greece and Rome just before they collapsed, largely from breakdown of the family. They put their children out to care by slaves; today we call it *day care* or *preschool*. The young soon became dependent on their peers for their standards and declined family values—as they do today. They rejected their parents whom they felt rejected them. When parents became old and ill, they relegated them to what amounted to *death houses*. That is what the Chinese frankly called them. We call them *nursing homes*. They serve a useful purpose, yet many aging parents find that children won't care for them, for sadly *the earlier you institutionalize your children, the earlier they institutionalize you.*

Leaders of all major U.S. churches, including Pope John Paul, embrace our formula in one way or another. We have been grateful for General Conference support. We do understand the fears of North American Division [NAD] school leaders that homeschooling causes declines in our church school system. However we have proven through cooperation with church schools that if they follow God's teacher-student work-study program, God guarantees success. So we have informed NAD leaders that our help is available to all schools through our *Malachi Movement.* And we are proving its success. It was our *mutual prophet* who inspired our research and *our mutual God* who turned it into the world's largest excelling school movement. It was God, not Moores who returned homeschools to prominence they enjoyed during America's first centuries when the U.S. led the world in functional literacy and generated the Industrial Revolution.

Universities such as Wisconsin and Indiana, among many, avidly recruit its creative, work-study-service students. Public, private and church schools profit by using their methods derived from God through the Bible and Ellen White.**[Deut 6:6,7; CG 26; 8T 226; etc.]** And they mesh precisely with replicated research.

At first the inter-university Moore Foundation team concluded that, where possible, children should be withheld from formal schooling until at least ages eight to ten. Then Elkind[3] warned against student burnout which has become pervasive in American schools, insisting that the earlier children start school the greater the likelihood of failure. Rohwer[4] agreed, basing his conclusions in part on investigations in 13 countries by Sweden's Torsten Husen. Husen confirmed Rohwer's unexpected interpretation of his research[5]. Rohwer, with deep concern for demands which reading and arithmetic place on unready minds, offered a solution:

"All of the learning necessary for success in high school can be accomplished in only two or three years of formal skill study. Delaying mandatory instruction in the basic skills until the junior high schools years could mean academic success for millions of school children who are doomed to failure under the traditional school system."

These findings may seem extreme to some who are conventionally oriented. Yet they are strongly supported by Scripture, history, research and common sense across America and in many countries around the world:

1. Ellen White who said children should be homeschooled until *maturity*. **[CG 26, 300, CH 177, CT165]** If you can't do that, enroll them in a school like a rightly-conducted homeschool. **[8T226]**

2. Ancient Israel's ages of maturity (12 for girls and 13 for boys, now *Bat Mitzvah* and *Bar Mitzvah*), which were "ages of responsibility," and until then, children remained at home with their families and learned how to earn a living.

3. U.S. 17th to 19th Century school entry ages of 10 to 14 when homeschools were dominant, and literacy was highest ever.

4. Researchers and analysts from Cal-Berkeley, Columbia, Cornell and Stanford who came up with ages within 10 to 14, or centering in junior high.

This solution would delay school entrance at least until the child is 10 to 13, ages which become landmarks. A Columbia study suggested the seventh grade as early enough for pressure to learn math.

Dr. James T. Fisher, then dean of American psychiatrists, confirmed this ideal in his 1950 autobiography, *A Few Buttons Missing:* His industrialist father sent young Jim "out west" at age 8 to learn from nature in the "great open spaces." At 13, his mother insisted he return to Boston to start school. He was unable to read or write. Yet he graduated from high school at 16. He thought he was a genius until he found that any "normal" child could do it, adding, "If a child could be assured of a wholesome home life and proper physical development, this might provide the answer to...a shortage of qualified teachers."[6]

In face of sound research and practice, and with the present and future health of children at stake, how can present trends toward earlier schooling be justified? They normally are not mature enough for formal studies until senses (vision, hearing, taste, touch, smell), coordination, brain development, and reasoning ability (cognition) are ready.[7] Swiss psychologist Jean Piaget reminded us 20 years ago in Geneva that the average [peer-oriented] American child does not reach adult-level cognition until about 15 to 20. Yet those who spend most of their time with their parents often achieve this maturity between 8 and 12.[8]

A century or more ago, John Dewey[9] challenged trends and called for school entry at age eight or later. A half century later, Skeels[10] proved that loving, though retarded, teenagers made remarkably good teachers. A quarter century after Skeels, Geber[11] demonstrated that mothers in the African bush brought up children who were more socially and mentally alert than youngsters of the elite who could afford preschool. Warmth was the key. Still later, Mermelstein and others[12] proved that, at least until ages nine or ten, children who went to school did no better than those who did not attend school. And today Yale pediatrician and neurologist Sally E. and Bennet A. Shaywitz, talk of lifting pressures from our kids instead of rushing them into school.[13] At Stanford, where we directed one of our research projects, the project's Hoover Institution's De Rebello (unpublished data, January 1985) reported that in India dropouts who find employment are ahead of their peers in mental and social perception.[14]

Few conventional educators understand or accept this kind of talk. We do not understand fully the damage or frustration nor denial of children's natural rights to explore their interests freely under warm adult guidance, nor the value of warmth as a learning motivator, nor yet the tutorial method which historically has never been equaled. A UCLA study of 1,016 public schools found teachers averaging about seven minutes daily in personal exchanges with their students.[15] This would not even allow one or two personal responses for each student. And those were not all warm. In contrast, our counts of daily responses in typical home schools ranged from over 50 to nearly 300.

We should not be shocked then by the Smithsonian Report[16] on the history of genius which offered a three-part recipe for high achievement, including 1) much time with warm, educationally-responsive parents and other adults, 2) very little time with peers, and 3) a great deal of free exploration under parental guidance. Study director Harold McCurdy concluded:

> "...the mass education of our public school system is, in its way, a
> vast experiment on reducing...all three factors to a minimum;
> accordingly, it should tend to suppress the occurrence of genius."[17]

In the late 1990's, before the days of better state laws, we obtained all court-accepted standardized test scores of children whose mothers or fathers were arrested for teaching at home. Many parents were of low socioeconomic status with less formal education than usual, yet, the children averaged 80.1%, or 30 percentile ranks higher than the nation's average classroom child. Results vary, but one recent study sent to us by an Idaho legislator found the average homeschool child's composite score for all subjects in Idaho was 87% (88% in math and 89% in reading). Some of the credit for these high scores is believed due to the creative freedom Idaho grants to parents. Idaho, which only a few years ago was jailing parents for teaching their children at home now has, under the guidance of lawmakers Fred Tilman and Bob Forrey, one of the best laws in America.

Very young children do indeed learn very fast, as is commonly believed, yet usually in proportion to their maturity. The child who combines cognitive maturity with eight to ten years or more of free exploration has developed thousands of "learning hooks" and an ability to reason consistently which is impossible for the less mature child. Without this maturity, and confined to a classroom, the youngster often becomes anxious, frustrated, and eventually creatively crippled and learning disabled.

Sociability. The common assumption these days is that well-socialized children require the association schools afford. Replicable evidence clearly points the other way. Cornell studies[18] found that children who spend more elective time with their peers than with their parents until the fifth or sixth grades—about ages 11 or 12—will become peer dependent. Such "knuckling under" to peer values incurs four losses crucial to sound mental health and a positive sociability. Lost are self worth, optimism, respect for parents, and even trust in peers.

The loss to boys is of particular concern academically, behaviorally, and socially. Despite their widely-acknowledged delay in maturity, we demand their enrollment in school at the same ages as girls. In recent years, many reports suggest that boys are several times as likely as girls to fail, become delinquent, or acutely hyperactive. Perhaps most ominous are *Education Week* findings in American high schools that there are eight boys for each girl in classes for the emotionally impaired, and 13 for each girl are in remedial learning groups.[19] Self worth, male identity, and respect for women are lost—unfortunate outcomes especially in today's society.

A COMMON SENSE SOLUTION

We need more parent education, warm responsiveness and less institutionalizing of young children. In the modern renaissance of old-American homeschooling, thousands of over a million families have re-evaluated their child-rearing roles and awakened to the pleasure and blessings of warmly learning their children's developmental needs. The outcome is higher achieving, better behaving, self-directed children and a low-cost model which is being adapted by some American public schools. We might reflect on the glory of our industrial revolution and literacy of our early centuries when homeschools led American

44

education. The most successful family-directed programs are a far cry from the common homeschool concept of moving typical formal studies into the home by video, correspondence or other colorfully advertised modes. Instead, they combine study with creative and entrepreneurial manual work and home and community service.

While insisting on strong learning tools—grammar, math, spelling, writing—the child's study focuses primarily on his own interests. For example, when a Houston 10-year-old boy, burned out and suicidal—but hooked on motorcycles—shifted to a simple unit on transportation he was shortly covering the world, including everything from jinrickshas in Japan and caribou carts in the Philippines to camels in the Middle East and jetliners in America, England and France. He learned sociology via cultures and folkways; math from costs and depreciations and writing by writing letters to manufacturers and individuals, from Harley-Davidson engineers to Boeing and its test pilots. He was shortly into physics and chemistry from internal combustion motors to weather forecasting.

Such key Head Start founders as University of Chicago's Benjamin Bloom and chief psychologist Glenn Nimnicht called the home the best learning nest and parents as the best teachers.[20,21] And in both physical health and behavior—in exposure to disease (*Wall Street Journal*, Sept. 5, 1984) and to negative aggressive acts—the home is 15 times as safe as the average day care center.[21]

Several suggestions can help us improve the mental and emotional health of our children, *as much as possible*:

1) More of home and less of formal school;

2) More free exploration with the guidance of warm, responsive parents and fewer limits of classrooms and books;

3) More concern for readiness for learning and ability to think and less training to be simple repeaters;

4) More attention to educating parents and less to institutionalizing young children;

5) More and higher priorities to child-rearing and fewer to material wants; and

6) More old fashion chores—children working with parents—and less attention to rivalry sports and amusements.

To educators and parents paralyzed by convention, such ideas may appear prosaic or dull—like the sandy backyard Al Hafed left. Yet, everyone likes diamonds, and that backyard can be an exciting pad. Anything else may be more child abuse than education.

SUMMARY

The *Journal of Adventist Education* has done a great service by bringing together some of the most remarkable studies on the human brain.[22]

A leader is Linda Bryant Caviness, whose recent study should be in the hands of every Adventist pastor, and health and educational professional.[22, 23]

REFERENCES

1. Moore, RS: *School Can Wait*. Provo, Utah, Brigham Young University Press, 1979, 1982, 1999, seven printings pp 175-186. *Better Late Than Early*, Readers Digest Press, 1975. Both books available through Moore Foundation, Box 1, Camas, WA 98607

2. The Adult Performance Level Project (APL). Austin, Texas, University of Texas, 1983.

3. Elkind D: The case for the academic preschool: Fact or fiction? *Young Child* 1970;25:180-188.

4. Rohwer WD Jr: Prime time for education: Early childhood or adolescence? *Harvard Educ Rev* 1971;41:316-341.

5. Letter to R. S. Moore, Nov. 23, 1972.

6. Fisher JT, and Hawley LSH: *A Few Buttons Missing*. Philadelphia, JB Lippincott, 1951, p 14.

7. R.S.Moore, *Ibid*.

8. Quine, David, University of Oklahoma. Home: 2006 Flat Creek, Richardson, TX 75080

9. Dewey J: The primary education fetish. *Forum* 1898;25:314-328.

10. Skeels HM: *Adult Status of Children with Contrasting Early Life Experiences: A follow-up study*. Chicago, University of Chicago Press, 1966.

11. Geber M: The psycho-motor development of African children in the first year, and the influence of maternal behavior. *J Soc Psychol* 1958;47:185-195.

12. Mermelstein E, Shulman LS: Lack of formal schooling and the acquisition of conversation. *Child Dev* 1967;38:39-52.

13. Shaywitz, Sally E. and Bennet A., Telephone call from Yale University, New Haven, Co. Called to congratulate us on research.

14. DeRebello D. Unpublished data, January 1985.

15. Goodlad J: A study of schooling: Some findings and hypotheses. *Phi Delta Kappan* 1983;64(7):465.

16. McCurdy HG: The childhood pattern of genius. *Horizon* 1960;2:33-38.

17. Bronfenbrenner U: *Two Worlds of Childhood: US and USSR*. NY, Simon and Schuster, 1970, pp 97-101.

18. March 14, 1984, p. 19

19. Bloom BS: *All Our Children Learning*. Washington, DC, McGraw-Hill, 1980.

20. Hoffman BH: Do you know how to play with your child? *Woman's Day* 1972;46:118-120.

21. Farran D: Now for the bad news...*Parents Magazine* 1982 (Sept):80.

22. December 2000/January 2001 issue.

23. Caviness, Linda Bryant, *Educational Brain Research as Compared with E. G. White's counsels on Education.*. Doctoral dissertation Andrews University. Sept. 2000.

And thou shalt teach...
Diligently unto thy children...
When thou sittest in thine house...
Walkest by the way...
Liest down...and risest up.
                —Deut. 6:7

CHAPTER 9

GOD'S GREAT EDUCATIONAL ANSWER THROUGH ELLEN WHITE

Backdrop. *Russell Conwell's famed account of Farmer Al Hafed's blind pursuit of treasure, without checking the research is an almost perfect parallel with the modern early childhood education [ECE] movement. It is easy to talk of values without understanding or appreciating them, and debate solutions as if legendary. We sell our souls for answers when they are in our own "back yards." What more appropriate gems are there than God's words through His modern prophet, Ellen White? How earnestly do you study them? As though your eternal life depended on them? It does.*

It's an amazing, eternal miracle when we *diligently* obey. God's blessings *overtake* us and make us "the head and not the tail."[Deut 28:1-13] But where do we find the instructions—the *maps* to His Treasure? He says "Believe in the Lord your God, so shall ye be established; believe His prophets, so shall ye prosper.[2 Chron. 20:20] So, to prosper, do *exactly* as He says. We must, to the best of our abilities know His prophets and obey them. Yet to obey, we will often have to turn from conventional ways that *seem* natural and good, but in fact are appalling in their outcomes. Moses told parents nearly 3500 years ago to keep their children close to them—as Mary and Joseph did with Jesus nearly 1500 years later. [Deut. 6:6,7]

God's modern messenger, Ellen White [EGW] said nearly 3500 years later, "Children should virtually be trained in a home school from the cradle until maturity."[CG 26] But when is "maturity?" Israel had "*bat mitzvah*"—12 for girls, and "*bar mitzvah*"—13 for boys. Modern research from Andrews [AU], Loma Linda University [LLU] and Stanford to Cornell and Columbia agree. Cal-Berkeley's William Rohwer insists if we wait until junior high school for formal schooling, we'll save millions of children from learning failure.

Yet some 600 years after Moses, "Fathers and mothers in Israel became indifferent to their obligation to God [and] their children." [ED 45-7] So God told Samuel to build schools where teachers and students joined in learning a balance of study, work and service they should have mastered at home. In 1907 we were told, **"With us as with Israel..., success in education depends upon fidelity in carrying out the Creator's plan."** [ED 50]

Testing God. Knowing some parents wouldn't or couldn't do this, God gave us modern schools of the prophets—church schools—to follow His balanced plan where he told all teachers, **"Several hours each day should be devoted to working with the students in some line of manual training...In no case should this be neglected."[CT211]** If there were any doubts about the time to be devoted to each, there should be more work than study. [FE41, MM 81] Here are God's sands that guarantee more than diamonds.

These words meant much to us in 1968 after experimenting with His instructions many years here and overseas, in public, SDA and other schools, colleges and universities. After a stint with the U.S. Office of Education, General Conference leaders joined us in forming a research foundation at Andrews and Loma Linda mostly to do efficiency research for the Church. The GC treasurer and two vice-presidents, along with a distinguished bi-racial lay SDA board, were overseers (a law dean, Harvard professor, industry heads, IRS regional chief, state department of education chairman, physicians, et al). With the help of AU and LLU scholars, we studied such areas as education, evangelism, finance, health, nutrition, management and personnel. Out of that group also came a college and health center at Weimar, CA., another at Black Hills in South Dakota, one at Hartland in Virginia, and an array of lifestyle centers. Weimar and Black Hills are members of GC's services and industries (ASI).

Yet in the Foundation's widest-ranging and most influential study, God used scholars from AU, LLU, Universities of Colorado (Med School), Massachusetts, Stanford, World Health Organization, the Smithsonian, *et al* to see how early schooling trends and EGW counsel fared with sound research. When God gave our reports to *Reader's Digest* (without our knowledge), *Time*, major talk shows, journals and newspapers and other media, a home-education focus emerged that became America's largest successful education movement involving millions of families. It was conventional since the 17th to 19th centuries when home education was normal, and literacy and creativity were highest in our history. It birthed the Industrial Revolution.

It's inescapable: all homes are teaching homes for good or bad. In America we have known for centuries that, wisely used, home teaching helps all classroom schools that work closely with them, lowering debt, increasing enrollment and building character. It is a soul winner that earns money and friends. A Midwest SDA church school had six students when it began helping homeschools; the next year its full-time enrollment was 13. In the same year that we write this book it has been our privilege under God—using the methods in this book—to revive and place on a debt-free operation at least ten schools in America and overseas.

When some education leaders still felt it would hurt SDA enrollments to work with homeschools, one affiliated Canadian ASI church school netted $100,000 yearly "mothering" 500 homeschool families. Early in the Movement when we needed this kind of cooperation in the greater Chicago area, and for one reason or another our SDA academies were not available, we turned to interdenominational Christian Liberty Academy, and gave notice in our book *Home Grown Kids*. At last report, it was serving 25,000 families—not perfect but helpful. And we help many public schools.

Since the homeschool movement is alive and well in North America, and is well underway from Australia and Japan to Europe and Africa, a number of us have piloted a new educational movement that meets the call of God to answer in the manner of Isaiah 54, 58 and 60: To arise and shine, enlarge, lengthen our cords, strengthen our stakes and cry aloud the Elijah message of Malachi 4:5,6. Our target no longer is centered on homeschools, much as we have been blessed. It now targets all families and all schools. We call it *The Malachi Movement*.

AN EXCITING HISTORY

In summary: Home teaching dominated American and Canadian education from the 1600s to the late 1800s, including the Industrial Revolution. American literacy was above 90%. Today it's 50%. Whether or not they know EGW, the best of homeschools heed her readiness recipe and study-work-service balance in a world-leading mastery of low stress, highly creative, noble behavior and low-cost education for English-speaking countries, now being readied for other languages.

The Initiators. Although we are widely credited as grandma and grandpa of the modern homeschool movement, the truth is that God used Ellen White to inspire it, and *Harper's* and *Reader's Digest* to spread it around the world in July and October 1972 respectively to more than 52,000,000 readers. The U.S. Congress, Republican and Democratic, *volunteered* more money. We owe a lot to people like Sandi Scully Ratliff who as wife of a pastor gave Dr. James Dobson a copy of our Reader's Digest Press book *Better Late Than Early*. He read it carefully, gave up his early school favor, and has aired us for 15 years. Others—Quiet Hour, 3ABN-TV, VOP, Moody, Thomas Nelson, Word, et al—have raised our interview numbers to thousands. Out of hundreds of syndicated articles such as United Press, Associated Press and other services, very little was initiated by us. Australia offered its main weekly television hour, "Monday Conference;" Erma Bombeck gave her funny column, and Random House Dictionary coined a new word: "homeschool."

The Followers: Roman Catholic and most prominent Protestant schools, angry in the Movement's early days, are now enthusiasts. Baptist, Presbyterian, Episcopal, Synagogues and most Bible Churches welcome it. The Pope and cardinals recently endorsed this SDA ideal; noting its evangelistic potential, they offer curriculum help for little or no cost. Al Hafed's hopelessness mirrors

America's choice of educational direction, but, judging from the first 25 exciting years of the home education movement home teaching has, under God, enjoyed a remarkable renaissance.

ANSWERS TO SOME COMMON QUESTIONS

Achievement. We have already cited Idaho and other examples. Homes that average highest usually reflect Ellen White's God-given advice: (1) balance of study, work and service, (2) delay formal school, (3) a focus on student interests, aptitudes and abilities, (4) much less stress and (5) few if any legal problems. This is widely called "The Moore Formula," but it is really God's Formula through EGW. And we tell our seminars that our success and high scholarship records came from God through her.

Sociability. An Andrews/Massachusetts University team found that 1) 77.7% of homeschoolers are in America's highest quartile, and 2) warm, responsive parents make good teachers regardless of education level. Smithsonian and Cornell studies on genius and values would limit association with peers— who are seldom models for positive behavior, but promote negative socialization.

Maturity and Cognition. Recent studies find that advanced levels of cognition strengthen achievement and sociability. This was proved by the Christ-child when he outreasoned the rabbis at age 12. So today, those following EGW counsel, SDA or no, often reach mature adult cognition by 8 to 12, seven years ahead of the usual 15 to 20.

Methods. Top homeschools target students' worthy interests, using sharp tools in language, math and phonics in mostly informal ways. They tailor them to each child with unique projects, games and books and much freedom to explore in history, sciences and arts, as the Smithsonian suggests, and EGW affirms. Teachers and students jointly use manual skills instead of rivalry games and amusements; the older help the younger, and the stronger the weaker. [ED 286] They run home industries, write checks to pay bills, manage the home, help the needy. This joins sound research in a harmonious mental, physical, and spiritual balance, fits programs to student aptitudes and abilities, and teaches sound habits of diet, exercise, recreation and sleep.

Research. The Movement that started with research rooted in the Bible and Ellen White writings, is a world leader in readiness factors like brain development, cognition, hearing, vision, cognition and sociability and has helped to change state and local laws to favor the best of learning. It is a redemptive reminder of homeschoolers like Abraham, Isaac, Jacob and Jesus; of America's George Washington, Abraham Lincoln, George Washington Carver and Thomas Edison; and of Canada's William Van Horn, Simon Fraser and Alexander Graham Bell. But much remains to be done both in home and conventional education.

Boys trail girls in maturity, yet in one of the most pervasive forms of child abuse, are forced to enroll—or start formal school at home—at the same ages. In schools, remedial classes average thirteen boys to every girl, many wretchedly on Ritalin. Ridiculed, they sense failure, family rejection and become peer dependent—a social cancer that courts delinquency, alcohol, illicit sex, drugs, violence and other evils for which God-given research and EGW sands have answers! See Chapter 8 for a synopsis of our research as published in the *Journal of School Health.*

Heroes and Heroines. After finding that her children needed her badly, Astronautic Electronics Engineer Helen Jackson gave up her NASA promotion to be the first black female in space. She was also Texas' class-action heroine in a suit that won parent rights to teach. Since then her children have won scholarships, including AU, Oakwood and University of Tennessee, Knoxville (in chemical engineering) and Weimar. Her husband, John, shares her heroism.

Scholarships. The Formula produces a high percentage of major scholarships. All of the 11 Kevin Harrington children of age have enjoyed major scholarships, four of them with major grants from Loma Linda University, others from Stanford, Universities of Idaho, Southern California, etc. Three won prizes otherwise awarded only twice in UI history; three more plan to join their sisters and brothers at Loma Linda University Medical School. Many are National Merit Scholars, Alaskan Barnaby Marsh became a Rhodes Scholar, and has stayed on to become a professor there. Harvard considers EGW types "a luxury." Stanford at this writing has announced that its homeschoolers score high in math and set a pace for excellence.

Others do well at Armed Forces Academies. For years the U.S. Air Force Academy arranged for us to guide homeschool applicants for all U.S. academies. God is responsible for all of this. His methods should be the first order of our educational days. His accreditation is of the highest order.

Entrance Age and the Law. After 25 years of legislative and court battles, in all of the United States and New Zealand and much of Australia, Canada and Japan, most parents have rights to teach at home. In 25 years no Moore Academy family has been in court. Although most top homeschool families delay formal instruction until 8 to 13, their children learn from birth, work from infancy, and earn a creative living by early teens. Yet from Cal-Berkeley and Stanford to Columbia and the Smithsonian, scholars say, "Whether at home or school, give your children a balanced education that targets their interests, and don't formalize it until junior high!" And God blesses. Yet few of us seem to know. Maybe, like Al Hafed, we haven't looked in our own back yards.

An hour's industry will do more
to produce cheerfulness, suppress
evil humours and retrieve your
affairs than a month's moaning.
> —Benjamin Franklin

CHAPTER 10

THE TEACHER-STUDENT WORK-EDUCATION PROGRAM[1]

Backdrop. *These are times when we need every legitimate method, device, technique or invention we can lay our hands on in order to prepare our youth for the challenge of eternity when they will minister in the vast courtrooms of the King of the Universe. But many of us may be either overlooking, or neglecting in part, the greatest all-round educational resource of all. And this treasure, like acres of diamonds, lies in our own backyard—so rich it was shared with Adam before the fall.[2] Satan would have us believe this diamond is ordinary dirt. But God's double-acting design for man, the privilege of labor, is defensively a safeguard against temptation, and offensively brings such dignity, nobility and eternal riches as none other can bestow.[3] It was designed to make us distinctive, leaders, the head and not the wagging tail, trying to please the world.* **This is God's way for parents and teachers to mentor our children.** *When parents and teachers realize the blessings of work with young people, they are excited.*

In the early 1980s, Pastor Dick Matthews called us from Corning, California,about a school that was one of the most troubled we ever faced. The economy was depressed nationally. Gasoline prices had sky-rocketed. This hurt Corning, for it was an industrial center for recreational vehicles [RVs]. Out of a 100 members, the local SDA church had only three regularly-employed. The junior academy of 28 students was in debt to the Conference of between $20,000 and $30,000. So the educational director ordered the school closed. The pastor and the school board objected, and were willing to try "anything." At that point Matthews called us.

In order to avoid confrontation, He set up a wood-toy industry in his own double garage with the help of laymen under the leadership of Entrepreneur David Johnson, and did well under God's blessings from the start. Yet since Johnson was a beekeeper, among several occupations, they were soon also making wood-and-screen packages for shipping bees.

In setting up their assembly line, they carefully evaluated each student. They chose one of Corning's worst rebels, a very able 10-year-old boy, as quality-control officer. Soon the industry was making most of California's bee packages, and had turned the rebel into a champion whose grades went from Ds and Fs to Bs. They paid off the entire debt and the operating costs for the new year. It was a thrilling test of God's Deuteronomy 28 promises.

Among the most exciting stories in our professional lives have been those from Kabiufa, New Guinea, not far from where I served in World War II. For years they have raised vegetables for the hotels of Port Moresby, and flown them down several times a week. And there was Riverside Farms in Africa, among many others in that great continent. And it was a great privilege to consult with Little Creek and to visit Laurelbrook in Tennessee, and many more. However, among my deepest disappointments was having to turn down Dr. E. A. Sutherland's invitation to replace him at Madison College also in Tennessee. But I had an imperative reason. We were at that moment carrying out the almost identical program you have been reading about in earlier chapters of this book.

*Visits to the Leland Straws and the Little Creek family were always fulfilling moments with happy, self-controlled students and teachers who knew they were on God's target—teacher and student **together**—to reach otherwise unreachable goals. We find the same vibrant emotions as we write this book as we train 1000 godly teams for our **Malachi Movement** [Mal 4:5,6] to carry this message around the world at the request of General Conference educational leaders. If you would like to share, whether part time or full time, active or retired, in an excellent paying seminar market, tell us! Our standards are strict, but not impossible. **When you see it in operation and do it, you will likely say, "Where have we been? Why haven't we done this before?" And our Savior will embrace you!***

The need—at all levels, for everyone. It makes no difference on what level we are teaching; God's plan takes in all students and all teachers:[4] (a) "The approval of God rests" upon children who work in the home environment.[5] (b) Some of His most specific instruction was addressed to our *intermediate* schools which were then roughly equivalent to the function of what is now a junior college.[6] And (c) His counsel to "exercise *equally* mental and the physical powers" would make labor at all levels important.[7] This includes the college, for there the mind is called to greatest effort and perhaps needs even more physical work in order to provide a balance.[8] We say "physical work," for we are instructed that it is "much preferable" to play.[9] In fact, the student's education *is not complete* if he is not taught how to work.[10]

Heaven's panacea. Work education automatically solves more personal and institutional ills than any dozen ordinary education inventions. And if, in the face of temptations we do not use this cure-all, we will be "held to account."[11]

"For evils that we might have checked we are just as responsible as if we were guilty of the acts ourselves."[12] Many will face this in the Judgment.

What evils will be checked by a balanced work-study program? you may ask. Let us consider them from a positive point of view:

Equality of man. One of the greatest unsolved problems in most schools is the psychological conflict between the "smart set" and the working student. Nothing will establish high campus morale, lift school spirit and erase suspicion sooner than a work program for *all*. At school, manual work is a great leveler. Whether wealthy or poor, cultured or unrefined, students thus learn better their true value to God—the equality of man.[13] They learn practical religion.[14] They find "that no man or woman is degraded by honest toil."[15]

Health of body and mind. Balanced living with a work program always brings better health: (a) equalizes circulation of the blood,[16] (b) counteracts disease,[17] (c) keeps every organ in running order,[18] (d) helps toward mental and moral purity.[19] In fact, rich or poor, work is needed for health.[20] Health cannot be preserved without it,[21] nor can a fresh, vigorous mind, healthy perception and well-balanced nerves.[22] Students should, as a result of this program, leave our schools in better health than when they entered, more elastic in spirit, vigorous in thought and better able to discern what is truth.[23]

Strength of character and depth of knowledge. All noble character qualities and habits are enhanced by such a program.[24] *Purity* is impossible without it.[25] *Industry* and *firmness* are better taught this way than by books.[26] It develops principles of *thrift, economy* and *self-denial,* as well as an *understanding of the value of money.*[27] It inculcates *self-reliance,*[28] *ingenuity,*[29] and builds *steadfastness of purpose, leadership* and *dependability* through practical business experience.[30] Through care of tools, and work area, the students also learn *cleanliness, neatness* and *order*, and respect for the property of others, both personal and institutional.[31] And they will be filled with tact and *cheerfulness*, with *courage, strength,* and *integrity*.[32]

Common sense and self control. Such a balanced program also brings with it level-headedness, because it strains out selfishness, builds the qualities of the golden rule. *Common sense, balance, close observation*, and *independent thought*—rare qualities these days—add up quickly in a work program.[33] *Self-control*, "the highest evidence of nobility of character," is better taught through the balanced program of God than through the textbooks of man.[34] If students and teachers engage in manual work together, they will "learn how to gain control of self, how to work together in *love* and *harmony*, how to conquer difficulties."[35]

Efficiency for student and teacher. In a well-run work-education program the student learns to economize time through system, *accuracy, thoroughness* by making every move count.[36] His *nobility* is revealed in his *faithfulness*, "a worker that needeth not to be ashamed."[37]

54

But the greatest efficiency which such a program brings to the school seems at first a mystery, for it is the reaping of the blessings of God.[38] Discipline problems become scarce, scholarship is enhanced. Criticism dissipates, unity and higher spiritual tone are soon evident. The cry for entertainment and freer dating abates and the true missionary spirit fills the vacuum, attended with sharper, clearer minds and vibrant, healthier bodies. God *tells* us so; educational leaders of the world verify it; and, for skeptical minds, science proves it! Why should we lag?

The teacher spends much less time in administrative committees remedying problems which are now *prevented* through God's own therapy. He deals with minds which are "quickened" and filled with "wisdom from above."[39] Don't underestimate this miracle of efficiency which God performs in dedicated minds. Students and teachers working in a balanced program actually accomplish far more mental labor in a given time than those who restrict their schedules to study alone.[40]

Before the National Education Association of America became a labor union, it strongly favored work-study programs at all levels. Evelyn Waterman wrote in the *NEA Journal* (January 1958, p. 34): "We who work with and supervise...working boys and girls are proud of their accomplishments both in school and out and feel that they do as well as those who attend all day." We did a nationwide study of public and church schools in 1958-59 that strongly supported Waterman's conclusions. *Education Summary* published in September 27, 1959 and Columbia Broadcasting System gave it a special report.

Evangelism. Physical labor is a key to missionary work. When students work daily with teachers, their appetite for sports and amusements declines and they become missionary workers, for the Holy Spirit will have an opportunity to work.[41]

IMPLEMENTING THE PROGRAM

Initiating such a program which conflicts with bindings of tradition requires most careful education—before legislation. Here are some suggestions:

1. Take your board and faculty with you step by step. Study and pray with them earnestly, to discern systematically, both principle and methods. Every board and staff member should be thoroughly familiar with God's plan through Ellen White for joint student and teacher work-study-service programs in our schools. All should have an acquaintance with her operational books on education such as *Child Guidance, Counsels to Parents, Teachers and Students; Counsels on Diets and Foods,* and *Fundamentals of Christian Education,* and it would be well for all board members of health institutions to have a mastery of *Medical Ministry*."

2.   Give those in opposition a chance to study and report fully; often they later become your best cooperators; *and you may learn from them, too*!

3.   Leading students should also be brought into the planning, making sure that they study and understand the basic principle underlying every facet of your program. Open the financial records to them.

4.   After studying all aspects thoroughly, proceed cautiously, setting up necessary committees and coordinators, delegating commensurate authority as you place responsibility. Make sure that every teacher has specific supervisory responsibility in some phase of the manual activities.

5.   Consider such vital items as teacher loads, schedules, equipment, etc. Planning details thoroughly, but reserving enough flexibility so that you will not be alarmed if you make a mistake. (Remember that the finer details of implementation may be as different between schools as are the personalities of the schools themselves.)

6.   Make program educational—both for character and for vocational development. Treat the work program as any other study. Give academic credit where appropriate. Utilize rainy days for discussion time. Make sure that you never lose sight of the objective of teaching each student a trade insofar as possible. (Read Ed 218)

7.   Be sure that *all* teachers and *all* students participate. If even one is excepted, the program will be weakened. Unless it is clear that the student is engaging in systematic supervised work elsewhere, do not accept cash in lieu of work requirement.

8.   If the students are gathered for brief prayer before the daily work program, they may learn to understand better that they are working *with* God, and will be more alert to His blessings.

9.   When developing your public relations materials and when enrolling students, be sure to make clear the basic elements of the school program and why; then place the enrollment on an *elective* and *privileged membership* basis as with an exclusive club. In such an organization the member elects to "uphold and advance the principles and policies of the organization" as long as he desires to remain a member. Let the enrollee sign such a statement. Such a procedure stimulates a sense of personal and institutional pride and places the school in a desirable position when and if questions arise regarding the implementation of regulations.

10. Avoid anything that smacks of extremism, radicalism; return, if necessary, and go over the entire ground again in order to avoid this deadly trap insofar as possible. Insofar as practicable avoid the use of such trite expressions as "the Blueprint," "the program." Students are quick to note and tire of this. *Proceed with certainty and without apologetics. Confidence inspires confidence. Success will then breed success.*

56

QUESTIONS OR CHALLENGES YOU MAY HAVE TO FACE

1. *It's strictly against the customs and tradition of our country!*

The question here is, "Whom do we follow?" Satan and his binding traditions? Or God? The balanced program is working efficiently today in some of the most traditionally hidebound countries in the world. (See 6BC 1056 on Acts 5:29.)

2. *What will the governmental or other accrediting agencies say?*

Remember, we must first be accredited with heaven. In any event, the occasion is unlikely to arise around the world in which such an agency, fully informed, will not laud our objectives and approve our program—provided we show real effort and ingenuity in implementing them. These agencies usually judge you on how you are carrying out *your* objectives, not theirs!

3. *Won't it overload our teachers?*

Effort should be made to lighten the load of teachers whose work is primarily didactic (history, mathematics, etc.) so that they will have time for physical work with students. However, lowered committee (discipline, etc.) hours that invariably come with the balanced program will be real load lighteners.

4. *What if the teachers don't cooperate?*

Have you taken them with you in careful, systematic study of the principles, methods and instruction involved? If you have and they still do not cooperate, examine possible errors in your assignment of their place in the program (i.e., a painter assigned to work on the farm). If all possible has been done and cooperation has not been achieved (which will be a rare occasion), it might be necessary to arrange a transfer. As a preventive measure all new teachers should be thoroughly informed about the school program, and be expected to make clear where they stand, *before* employment.

5. *What if the students don't cooperate?*

It may be that they have not been well enough informed. Let them sign a pledge at the time of their application indicating their determination to uphold and advance the spirit, aims and program of the school or college. If later they do not cooperate, show them their pledge; remind them of the basic principles involved. If they do not then cooperate, they automatically elect to leave.

6. *But what if we lose students?*

This fear has been voiced again and again. But in the history of such programs, carried out as God has specified, there has been nothing but prosperity in all aspects of school life including enrollments. This does not mean that we should not use every sound public relations device to educate our students and constituency. Remember, people are waiting to be challenged, willing to follow if we show them something different that is worthwhile.

7. *What if we have an unsympathetic principal or board chairman?*

First, pray. The Holy Spirit can open hearts better than you. *Second*, know what you are doing, and have the personal authority that comes from such knowledge. *Third*, be always ethical, utilizing proper channels, following the Bible injunction of going directly "to thy brother;" avoid pressure groups, for they don't open closed minds. *Fourth*, be sure you *educate* carefully, not too much at a time, providing scriptural and other authority and information in clear, organized form.

8. *Yes, but that takes a lot of faith!*

Yes, it does. For your comfort, instruction and encouragement be sure to read all of page 290 in **Patriarchs and Prophets**. Read carefully also the following texts. If we are to succeed we must step out as the Israelites did (Hebrews 11:20); take God at His word and He will open the way step by step (PP 290). Some may say, "This instruction is not for my time and place." These will find their reward outlined in Deuteronomy (Deut. 28:15-68) and elsewhere through the Bible. Others will take God at His Word and will do exactly as He has instructed. They will study, pray and systematically counsel together. These will just as simply and directly reap the amazing rewards He has just as specifically outlined. (Read carefully Deut. 28:1-14; Isa. 49:22, 25; Isa. 58; Isa. 60)

9. *What if we make a mistake in interpreting the Bible or Spirit of Prophecy?*

Once we have determined to establish our faith and follow the Master architect's blueprint we will ever realize that we need eternal wisdom. We will determine not to be extremists, and in all things be sure that we are able to give the principle, the basic reason, underlying our every policy and act (Read 1 Peter 3:15). We will ever pray as we continually study, that God will give us a balanced interpretation and a true application of Heaven's principles. This prayer, and systematic study must be shared by all members of the faculty and board. He will then help us cut through human elements, ever hewing to the clear line of truth. If we do our best, we may leave the rest to God.

10. *I am not sure we have the courage!*

To follow God's plan against human reasoning, tradition and ridicule, always takes courage. But this is the only sure way, for God sees not as man sees. Read the texts (1 Sam. 16:7). Like Abraham (Gen. 12:4), Moses (Ex. 14:15-22), Gideon (Judges 6:14), Jeremiah (Jer. 26), and the Saviour, our every step will be forward. For God may wait for us to step in and get our feet wet before He prepares the way across our Red Sea (PP 290). "Go forward" is His mandate. If we really believe in Him, we will!

11. *How long and how much work should be required?*

The principle here is balance between study and work. Furthermore, we are told that the mental and physical activities should be equalized (Read FCE 538, 146-147, 321-323; 7T 267; AH 508-509). If one is stressed more than another it is only safe to stress the physical. The specific number of hours to be spent depends upon age, weather, climate, etc. However, in speaking of intermediate schools, we have been instructed that "several hours each day should be devoted to working with the students in some line of manual training. In no case should this be neglected." (Read CT 211) This would normally imply at least three hours per day (see Webster). And it is also a fact that in student work programs, a work period of less than three to four hours at a time is in most cases impractical and uneconomical.

12. *Our schedule is too crowded for work!*

If this is true then you have things backward. Work makes study more efficient if we are to believe 3T 159. Regular PE and other credit may be given for work experience. Experience has proven that a study schedule arranged around a balanced work program is possible. Vice versa is not. Furthermore, teacher committee time and formal counseling will be greatly minimized.

13. *What do you do if your teachers don't have any manual skills you can utilize?*

Three things: (1) Teach them. This can be done through late afternoon, evening, or summer classes, on campus or off. (2) Let them practice on campus. (3) When employing new teachers, insure that they are manually qualified if possible.

14. *We don't have enough work facilities!*

Go slowly, imaginatively, starting with campus services and needs, gradually branching into agriculture and industries suitable to local markets, transportation, climate, level of student ability, etc. Agriculture is best if it can be arranged, and is particularly ordained of God (Read Isa. 28:24-26; 6T 177-179; Ed 219).

15. *But we just can't provide enough work and will go in the hole financially, trying to pay all those students.*

It has been proven by experience that if one proceeds cautiously but firmly there need be no financial dilemmas. Among other things: (a) See how much of the work at your school is being done by full-time workers which could with careful planning and instruction be done by students—greatly to their character advantage and the school's. (b) Consider the work as part of the education program—the most important part—and not for pay. This eliminates problems of labor laws and labor unions and much accounting. Share your financial statement with your students and teachers. (c) Work gradually on industrial development. (d) Read 6T 177; CT 315-316; Ed 221.

16. *Our school is in the city so that we cannot have such a program.*

This is a real problem where it has been found necessary to build in the city. But even here it can be arranged so that (a) the daily custodial work including care of equipment and school yard is done by students and teachers working together. This may greatly increase the sanitation standards of the school, as well as the much more important achievement of character building. (b) Arrange to have students report on physical work done at home or elsewhere, documented

59

by appropriate signatures. (c) There are many industries which can be operated in minimal facilities.

17. *But part of our students are working off campus.*

Good! If it is in constructive type of activity, do all you can to cooperate with them. If you are charging "work tuition," this is the only group who should be allowed to pay this in cash.

18. *How about students who live at home?*

If work cannot be provided on campus for non-dormitory students, a work-control system may be arranged with their parents or guardians whereby the administration is assured of the student's daily work program at home.

19. *What do you do with the physically disabled?*

In the first place, require a certificate from the *school* or *college physician* determining if the individual is incapacitated, and how much and how long. Provide work of an appropriate nature for those who are permanently disabled. Experience has proven that even blind students fit into the balanced program.

20. *How do you handle the program during inclement weather?*

That depends upon the kind of work—outdoor or indoor, sheltered or not—and the necessity of carrying on during such weather. In many cases there are rainy or snowy-day sessions in classrooms, where discussions are held and plans made on the whys and hows to improve the efficiency of their departments. Such educational periods are vital in a manual training program that is *vocational education* in the real sense of the word. Many industries with careful management can arrange for inside assembling (e.g. wooden toys) or cleaning and servicing buildings, painting, etc. This is especially practical if gyms double as industrial centers.

21. *Don't you believe in play?*

By all means there is no objection to play, properly conducted. But we have been repeatedly instructed on the primary importance of constructive manual work as a greater and more efficient builder of character. (CT 274-275; FE 73; AH 499)

22. *But won't it get old?*

God's standard is higher than the highest human thought can reach. The balanced work-study program is a pioneering adventure in this day and age. As long as we keep the pioneering spirit, looking ever upward, it will never "get old." In fact, experience shows that with reasonable guidance and leadership, the success cycle becomes more and more full bloom. The program will fail only when vision is lost and expediency is substituted for principle.

23. *Will we have enough time to study?*

If we regulate study hours (CT 83-84; MH 240) and provide physical taxation equal to mental, God will make up the difference in mental ability so that much more will be accomplished in less time (3T 159; Ed 46; 6T 180; FE 44). Furthermore, if the teacher uses supervised study techniques wherever possible, particularly below college level, he can greatly increase his teaching efficiency. Repeated studies have proven this.

24. *What do you do for little children, Grades 1-4?*

Set up a chores program as described in *Adventist Education at the Crossroads*, pages 139-148, Pacific Press, or write to Moore Foundation.

25. *But isn't this really just for "intermediate schools?"*

Ellen White clearly prescribes such programs for "all levels." General Conference Work-Study Guide (1963) so states, page 3. This applies even to the medical school (MM 81). The principle is the equalization of mental and physical powers (FE 41). The more study, then, the more work.

26. *Wasn't this plan really for another time?*

Read carefully *Education*, page 50: "With us as with Israel of old, success in education depends on our fidelity in carrying out the Creators plan. Also enjoy *Patriarchs and Prophets*, page 290. Our schools are to be more and more like the Schools of the Prophets (CT 186, 203, 282, 353, 548-549; FE 184, 223, 228, 290, 489; 6T 139, 142, 145, 152; 8T 230; MM 75). There the teachers and the students both earned their way by manual labor as did the Apostle Paul (6BC 1062-1063)—to do otherwise, says Historian Alfred Eidershein, was considered a "crime." (FE 97; Ed 47)

REFERENCES

1. This paper was originally prepared for the first North American Conference of Educational Secretaries, Superintendents and Supervisors, which we conducted in 1959 from the Potomac (now Andrews) University Department of Psychology and Education. We have repeatedly updated as of 1980 and 2001. All footnotes are important but especially read sources in parentheses in the sentences or when marked "Read". RSM

2. Gen. 2:15.

3. Prov. 10:4; 15:19; 24:30-34; 26:13-16; 28:19; FE 513; CT 273-180; AH 91; Ed 214

4. MM 75-81 (also: *General Conference Guide for Work Experience Education*, p. 3).

5. AH 288; CT 148.

6. CT 203-214.

7. AH 508-509; 7T 267; FE 321-323, 146-147; MM 77-81 (G.C. Work-Study Guide).

8. TM 239-245; MM 81; 6T 181-192; FCE 38; Ed 209; CT 288, 348; FE 38, 40.

9. FCE 73; CG 342.

10. CT 309, 274, 354; PP 601.

11. CT 102, 268; FE 277.

12. Eze. 3; DA 441; CG 236; PP 441; 2T 54; 3T 265.

13. FE 423, 35-36; 3T 150-151.

14. CT 279; 2T 24.

15. Ed 215.

16. 5T 98; CE 9; CG 343.

17. Ed. 215.

18. CE 9; CG 343.

19. CT 274.

20. 3T 157.

21. CE 183; 3T 155.

22. CT 295; 6T 180; Ed 209.

23. CD 9; CG 343; 3T 159; 6T 180.

24. PP 601; COL 334; DA 72; 6T 180.

25. Ed 209, 214; CG 465; CG 465-466; SG 131; DA 72; PK 645; PP 60, 214; FE 36, 40; CT 207; 2T 403; 4T 95; 6T 180.

26. PP 601; Ed 221.

27. 6T 208; CT 273; 6T 176; Ed 221.

28. PP 601; Ed 221; CT 308.

29. Ed 220; FE 315; LS 353.

30. CT 285-293; 3T 148-159; 6T 180.

31. 6T 169-170, 176; CT 211.

32. 3T 159; 6T 168-192; Ed 222; FCE 315.

33. Ed 220.

34. DA 301; Ed 222, 287-292.

35. E. G. White letter, July 8, 1903, to W. C. White.

36. Ed 222; FE 315-316.

37. 2 Tim. 2:15; FCE 315.

38. Deut. 28:1-13; Isa. 60.

39. Ed 46.

40. 6T 180; 3T 159, FE 44.

41. FE 290, 220-225; CT 546-547; 8T 230.

CHAPTER 11

GOD'S VIEW OF RIVALRY SPORTS AND AMUSEMENTS

Backdrop. *We are not talking here about simple competition. I'll never forget my quest 30 years ago for a Michelin SAS tire. My favorite tire man didn't have the size I needed, so he called a competitor a few miles away and arranged for me to buy it there. There is a stark difference between Golden Rule competition and team rivalry where both teams play to defeat each other.*

Children do need exercise. Let's see that they get it–work or play— with us where possible. Even better than games and of much greater permanent value, we repeat, teach them manual and business skills in work at home and in schools. And also remember that the mentoring provided by adults with children and youth, is God's wondrous design for wholesome leadership and power. In ancient Israel it was considered a crime for parents to bypass adolescence without their children learning a skill by which they could earn a living for life, whatever their ultimate vocational goal may be.

For play, a choose-up game of baseball without rivalry can be great fun. For example, exchange catchers the first inning, pitchers second inning, first basemen third inning, until you have gone through the team for nine innings: Everybody wins. Try the same principle for basketball. Or rotate around the net in volley ball. It teaches great personality and character skills.

Poet Ralph Waldo Emerson wrote, "The years teach much which the days never know." Biographer Carl Sandburg and Ellen White were more direct: We don't need to fear the future except as we forget how we were led in the past. If we obey God diligently here, we will honestly examine both our near and distant past, prepared to set aside our private but doubtful appetites and addictions and carry the day for truth.

If only all recreation were based on this principle, like sailing, so wondrously creative as you play or work with the winds. Or cross-country skiing which adds a high order of vigorous exercise. And although it may be dimly viewed by some, walking is considered by the American Physical Education Association to be the best *daily* exercise of all; and it affords superb conversation time.

Are we alarmist to suggest that society's future depends upon how we look behind the development of sports and deal with their principles?

One man's family sport history. My dad graduated from the ninth grade and the elite University of Hard Knocks. His only academic diploma was a G.E.D. at age 70. As Charles David Moore—he answered to either "CD" or "Charlie—he was the star pitcher on his Company's Baseball Team when he wasn't supervising shipments to the Orient from Standard Oil's big refinery at Richmond, CA, or leading the San Francisco Bay Area Baptist Young People's Union [BYPU]. Every week he packed his delicate young wife, us two boys, a big paper bag of home-made popcorn and a Thermos jug of lemonade and trolleyed us off to the amateur hard-ball park north of Oakland. I still marvel at the infinite patience of our dainty, feminine mom, Dorcas, with her big-kid spouse, but Mother was a faithful trooper. Our neighbors called her "an angel," said she lived up to her Bible name. On Dad's outings, her conscience only troubled her for the unwashed clothes and sink full of dishes she sometimes was forced to leave behind.

Calculating or Crazed. But Dad was a trooper, too: As a boy, from age nine he sold papers, washed dishes, split wood—like Abe Lincoln, Tom Edison, Isaac Newton, Johannes Kepler and George Washington Carver—anything to earn a few pennies and help his mother feed six mouths besides her own. His minister father had left home for another woman, Charlie was the only boy in the house. Yet he was more fortunate than many youth today. He was kept busy, and later kept Charles and me busy.

From early boyhood until he left Illinois for California and married pretty Dorcas, a box-maker's blue-eyed, auburn-haired daughter, his nose was glued to spindles at the famed Zion City lace factory. Some would say that he was poverty-bound in a sweat shop except for the few hours weekly he pumped air into the old pipe organ at Evangelist John Alexander Douay's big church or at Raymond Richey's—my namesake—big tents. But the boy today who has more than he needs of time and money and nothing constructive to do is more to be pitied. Work should always come first, then let sports give acceptance and relief.

Then mother died.

Although nearly nine-months pregnant, she had nursed Dad and us boys through the deadly "flu" plague of 1918-19 plus a scarlet fever bout for my brother Charles and me. Then a month after she birthed our little sister, Loraine, Mother's tired immunities gave way to exhaustion and death. And sent another angel, our wonderful Grandma Moore to replace our angelic mom.

But after mother lay down for a long sleep, dad spent more and more time with us, eventually bringing us on his building and paving crews at early ages, and systematically building us physically, mentally, and spiritually. From that day, reality began to rule, and baseball was largely elbowed from Dad's agenda.

One of the reasons for this was his acceptance of the Adventist faith which set Saturday baseball games aside. But while moderating his sports mania, he was forgetting that he had cultivated mine. But something happened that was a moderator for me: He surprised Charles and me one Sunday and took us, ages 12 and 10, down to Los Angeles' Wrigley Field to watch the Hollywood Stars play out San Francisco for the Pacific Coast Pennant. Frank Shellenback, my southpaw pitching idol, would be on the mound. Besides, it would be a double-header! Just think, two games in a day, and Frank Shellenback besides!" Dad was always like that, giving us double measure.

We watched with awe from the bleachers as Shelly coolly put away San Francisco's best in a close game. Sports reigned. Then in a crisis moment, the last half of the ninth inning of the second game as I recall, a Hollywood batter smashed a line drive down the left-field line. The San Francisco outfielder dove sensationally for the ball and apparently snatched it. But in fact he fumbled, deftly picked it up and held it high as if he had caught it, indifferent to the fact that his fraud lay bare before Hollywood fans in the nearby stands and even more clearly to us bleacher kids across the field. Indifferent, that is, until as sport scribes aptly wrote, " 'All hell broke loose' when the umpire thumbed the batter out."

I pounded on Dad's knee in disbelief. "Will they really let him get away with that?" He looked down, obviously ashamed, punished that he had brought us out to this melee. He shook his head in disappointment and personal defeat. Boos swelled to angry shouts and then pop bottles, cans, food and paper cascaded like meteor showers. Loud speakers blared to no avail. Tempers flared against San Francisco and their fans, although that City had nothing to do with it. Moments later sirens blew, the police took over the game, and Dad took us home. That was our first and last family outing at a professional game. But in true sports-fanatic form, it only intensified my addiction. Sports "fan" of course means fanatic." Never mind, my craze was now all but out of control, more urgent than money, clothes or food. Fanaticism is a desperate devil's mania mix of fervor, dogmatism, prejudice and intolerance. Ponder its fruits these days in politics, religion and sports, to name only a few. But absent divine love and devotion, it is hell-bent.

Sports was now all but dethroned.

My developing addiction was momentarily curbed one day years later when someone handed me a book about a Hall of Fame baseball star who insisted, "You've got to cheat to win." I couldn't believe it. Yet today's little league madness makes those teen games look like a knitting bee. True, some seem pure as driven snow, but when the costs of equipment and time are added to the anger or emotional turmoil of loss, or yet the spill-over into home chores, the panorama is not one designed to please Heaven. Although I was baptized and went to church, sports had a tighter hold on me than my Savior. I could hardly wait for sundown Saturday nights to get the Sabbath game scores. USC was my sports cathedral for no particular reason: For when my fascination shifted to football, I couldn't afford the games. And Dad, who didn't know a football from an ostrich egg, would no longer take me there if I saved the pennies. So I turned the radio knob to the big stations when no one was around, glued to sportsmaniacal nonsense.

And I was not alone. Nor would I be today with sports allegories and press tips increasingly pervasive in our church journals, pulpits and schools, apparently unaware that God views it as foremost in counteracting the influence of the Holy Spirit on our youth. [FE 220-30] No wonder EGW says God is grieved.

After a few years on active duty in World War II and some exchanging homework for Bible and Spirit of Prophecy reading during doctoral study, the alarming truth about sport ethics finally seized me. On a secular television discussion of our research out of Cincinnati, a Christian, Kyle Rote Jr., had joined us, a newly-retired all-pro quarterback from the Dallas Cowboys football team who was then deep into remaking families. I asked him what he thought about the effect on family values when two teams were praying just before playing for the national title. His answer was, "That's pretty futile." When I asked if there was any room for the Golden Rule in a game like that, he answered, "Not much."

AN INDIVIDUAL MATTER

We are sometimes asked, "Then how about individual rivalry?" That may depend upon the goal: To beat an individual, beat the field or on the other hand, to beat the clock or the tape measure—as in a mile run, broad jump or pole vault? Jim Ryun, one of our homeschool dads, is an example. He became the world's premier miler, the first to beat the four-minute mile. Now a congressman, Jim modestly allows that he had a goal: To run the mile in less than four minutes. So he "just disciplined" himself in what he ate, drank and in all he did as Paul advised. [1 Cor.10:31] He then ran his best races out of "sheer joy" as the same Paul and the Psalmist challenged ancient Hebrews [Hebrews 12:1 and Psalm 19:5]. Ryun prayed for no divine help against miler "enemies" but only for sound judgment to avoid emergencies or mistakes and reach his goal, with his mind set on time or distances rather than people.

While directing an international advanced study consortium [Chicago, Johns Hopkins, Southern Illinois, Stanford, Tulane and Wisconsin universities], I learned a lasting lesson about nations: With University of Chicago Dean Sol Tax, we co-hosted "The First World Conference on Mankind." There at the Kellogg Center I gleaned at age 53 a lesson that I should have learned better 40 years before, and if ingrained into all youngsters early on, would assure far greater understanding among world races and creeds: Those world philosophical leaders and statesmen unanimously held that all great faiths today share one healing principle, *The Golden Rule*. It weaves through nations a priceless thread, and is simple enough for a child to understand: "Do to others as you would have them do to you." Sharing the universality of this creed were delegates ranging from Mahatma Ghandi's partner from giant India to the prime minister of tiny Lesotho in southern Africa and the top leaders of the "First Nations" [Indians] in America and Canada.

It was from these roots that it remained for a Jewish delegate to deal my sports addiction the *coup d' grace*. We were discussing the principle of sports rivalry as in the Olympic games when he quoted St. Paul out of the Christian Bible. He noted that Paul borrowed it from Christ, then applied a gentle twist of his Hebrew scalpel in my Gentile soul: Paul's admonition to the Romans during that empire's sports hey-day. Said he, "Be ye kindly affectioned one to another, *with brotherly love, in honor preferring one another*." [Romans 12:10, KJV] Rivalry sports can't excel there.

Try this test: What if you are a champion baseball pitcher with a string of no-hitters under your belt, the most feared pitcher of your time? You are summoned to relieve in the last half of the ninth inning with two out and men jetted to second and third bases moments before by a sacrifice fly deep into center field. You know you can put that baseball on a dime from 60 feet with a curve, knuckler or the fastest ball in the game. Your coach sent his other ace to the showers and summoned you to face a young hitter of another race who, on a comeback trail, is batting above .500 for the series and likely to be named its most valuable player. His is praying to win the last and deciding game, and the count on him is three balls and no strikes. Your catcher and coach pray that you will "mix them up, but keep them low and inside."

But you recall the Apostle Paul's wise, selfless and noble interpretation of the Golden Rule which the pastor mentioned at your baptism last year...."in honor preferring one another." It's you or he, pitcher or batter, ace of pitching aces against the Series' most valuable player, ego and ego, contract negotiation against contract, expediency confronting principle. This slugger you know can and will lay a high and outside pitch out of the park, or at least drive a single over the infield to advance two men home and "cream" the last game and the series. Yet he is all but helpless on a low and inside pitch for which you are most feared throughout baseball. Your catcher calls for a low and inside ball just within the strike limits. How do you pitch? Are you loyal to Romans 12:10?

Crazy? Of course, by the world's measure, where it is a matter of person over principle. Yet if you know rivalry team sports worth a nickel and are honest as a penny, you will admit that not an ace in the space of a ball field will pitch that ball high and outside unless there is an earthquake or he stumbles over the rubber on the mound. That is for better or worse the nature of the "character-building" activities we toss at, or require of our youngsters daily at school, sand lot or Little League. Similar comparisons could be made for almost any team sport. The things I hate about it are my long-delayed reluctance to admit the truth—the greatest ideal of freedom—and the fear that if I tell the truth to any other fanatic, he will think I am crazy, too. How do *you* respond?

Would it be too arbitrary to trace the root causes of our sport and amusement syndrome to suggest that the road from the farm to the suburbs and the city— over the last century or so has been freely traveled without safeguards, and is reaching its *dead* end? The American farm population has dropped from 90% to 4% or less, and declines of literacy with it. Are we short on thoughtful leaders to arrange for constructive activities to replace farm chores in the lives of our heirs.

The passage from farm work to boredom and from responsibility to sports and passive amusements has brought thoughtless and unprincipled investments in gyms and ball fields to the exclusion of, and indifference to, apprenticeships and manual skills that built our nation, and self worth in its citizens. We are not saying at all that gyms or ball fields are bad, but that constructive manual work should be applied in much greater measure than sports, and teach how to earn a living as well as to shoot a basket. We laud corporate executives who today are educating for employability. Ted Fujimoto tells more in Chapter 14. Meanwhile, here is a quote from Portland OREGONIAN Sports Writer J.E. Vader (12/3/95):

On and off the field, young athletes learn, early and often, that they are special, that the rules don't apply to them. "If the referee doesn't see it, it didn't happen. If your grades...aren't great, well, someone will find a tutor or even change them (the grades) or it just doesn't matter."

For years, led by University of Chicago Chancellor Robert Maynard Hutchins and Harvard's late President James Conant, some schools slowed, and the University of Chicago terminated, rivalry sports. We've had our orders from God via EGW for well over a century. Yet our institutional records invite sports-writer ridicule:

The Associated Press headlined a mainland SDA university in intercollegiate basketball: "83-point defeat (103-20) is nothing new for the...team." It had more fouls than points, and more turnovers than fouls and points combined. The leading scorer had five points. And they had only one assist. [HONOLULU ADVERTISER, D12, Nov 25, 1997]

American Broadcasting Company TV news shamed an SDA academy team that won a city sports title then rebuked league officials for refusing to change award rites from Friday night.

I realized belatedly that rivalry was the evil that broke up heaven. There will be no rivalry there, no more in the place where we are going. If we do not clearly understand this and actively endorse and obey it, what chance do you think that we will have of being in a society where no rivalry exists? or would even want to be there?

If your youth insist that their greatest interest is sports, ask them how much of a living that will earn them as they grow into adult years. If you haven't read our book, *Minding Your Own Business,* I think you will find it will shortly pay for itself.* Read it with your children if they are around 8 or older. Tell them that freedom and authority come only by accepting responsibility, and then give them that responsibility as officers of the family circle and industries. Let them pay the family bills on the family checkbook and keep accounts. If they find that you made a mistake at the end of the month, give them an A-plus! No rivalry sport can compare with family chores and properly-managed home or school industries in building sterling, creative personalities, characters, and reverence for their Maker.

----

* For information, phone 800-891-5255 or e-mail moorefnd@pacifier.com.

FENCES
There will be no fences in Heaven,
No markers where your land meets mine.
There honesty smothers suspicion,
And faith lingers long on love's wine.

There will be no highways in Heaven,
No chance of collision up there.
No language nor cultural barriers,
No burdens of color to bear.

Nor will there be railroads in heaven,
So, no *other side of the tracks*.
The rich man is one with the orphan:
God's mansions have swallowed the shacks.

No!

There are no divisions in Heaven,
No curse of the property line.
Your vineyard will blend with my garden,
And love be the fruit of the vine.

-- RSM

68

An ordinary mind, well-disciplined, will accomplish more and higher work than will the most highly educated mind and the greatest talents without self-control.
—COL 335

CHAPTER 12

SELF-CONTROL
THE CERTAIN SOURCE OF BRILLIANCE

Backdrop. *So many of our students doubt their abilities to do great things for God, that I undertook this paper with Ellen White for the students of Andrews University in 1979. Yet students are even more fearful—and eager—in 2001. God made the mind. These are **His** promises below, abridged from that paper.*

Brilliance for all. God alone can measure the powers of the human mind. It was not His design that man should be content to remain in the lowlands of ignorance, but that he should secure all the advantages of an enlightened, cultivated intellect. Every man and every woman should feel that obligations are resting upon them to reach the very height of intellectual greatness. — 4T 413, Deut. 28:13.

The Brightest People. God requires the training of the mental faculties. He designs that His servants shall possess more intelligence and clearer discernment than the worldling, and He is displeased with those who are too careless or too indolent to become efficient, well-informed workers. — COL 333.

A New Mind. In the Bible the will of God is revealed. The truths of the Word of God are the utterances of the Most High. He who makes these truths a part of his life becomes in every sense a new creature. He is not given (inherently) new mental powers, but the darkness that through ignorance and sin has clouded the understanding is removed. The words, "A new heart also will I give you," mean, "A new mind will I give you." A change of heart is always attended by a clear conviction of Christian duty, an understanding of truth. He who gives the Scriptures close, prayerful attention will gain clear comprehension and sound judgment, as if in turning to God he had reached a *higher plane of intelligence*. — MLT 24.

Mind's Law: Narrow or Broad. It is the law of the mind that it will narrow or expand to the dimensions of the things with which it becomes familiar. The mental powers will surely become contracted, and will lose their ability to grasp the deep meanings of the word of God, unless they are put vigorously and persistently to the task of searching for truth. — CT 460, FE 127.

Mind's Law: High or Low. It is a law both of the intellectual and spiritual nature, that by beholding we become changed. The mind gradually adapts higher than his standard of purity or goodness or truth. If self is his loftiest ideal, he will never attain to anything more exalted. Rather, he will constantly sink lower and lower. The grace of God alone has power to exalt man. Left to himself, his course most inevitably will be downward. ---GC 555.

Intellect and the Bible. As a means of intellectual training, the Bible is more effective than any other book, or all other books combined. The greatness of its themes, the dignified simplicity of its utterances, the beauty of its imagery, quicken and uplift the thoughts as nothing else can. No other study can impart such mental power as does the effort to grasp the stupendous truths of revelation. The mind thus brought in contact with the thoughts of the Infinite can not but expand and strengthen. — Ed. 124.

Efficiency. A failure to study God's word is the great cause of mental weakness and inefficiency. In turning from this word to feed on the writings of uninspired men, the mind becomes dwarfed and cheapened. It is not brought in contact with deep, broad principles of eternal truth. The understanding adapts itself to the comprehension of the things with which it is familiar, and in this devotion to finite things it is weakened, its power is contracted, and after a time it becomes unable to expand. — CT 441 (Psalms 119:130).

Deep Thinking. Put your highest power into your effort. Call to your aid the most powerful motives. You are learning. Endeavor to go to the bottom of everything you set your hand to. Never aim lower than to become competent in the matters which occupy you. Do not allow yourself to fall into the habit of being superficial and neglectful in your duties and studies; for your habits will strengthen and you will become incapable of anything better. The mind naturally learns to be satisfied with that which requires little care and effort, and to be content with something cheap and inferior. There are, young men and young women, depths of knowledge which you have never fathomed, and you are satisfied and proud of your superficial attainments. If you knew much more than you do now, you would be convinced that you know very little. SD 106

Strong, Clear Thinking. It is the duty of every child of God to store his mind with divine truth; and the more he does this, the more strength and clearness of mind he will have to fathom the deep things of God. And he will be more and more earnest and vigorous, as the principles of truth are carried out in his daily life. — SD 327, (cf SD 322 and R&H, Sept. 20, 1881).

The Holy Spirit. Only the Holy Spirit of God can quicken the perceptive faculties. SDA 33.

Self Control and the Mind: Brilliance. Self-discipline must be more than eloquence or the most *brilliant* talents. An ordinary mind, well disciplined, will accomplish more and higher work than will the most highly educated mind and the greatest talents without self-control. — COL 335.

Speeding up Your Mind. God demands of you vigorous and earnest intellectual efforts, and with every determined effort, your powers will strengthen. Your work will then always be agreeable...you will know that you are progressing. You can either become...slow, uncertain, irresolute...so much so that the work of your life will not be one-half what it could be; or, your eyes fixed upon God, and your soul strengthened by prayer, you can overcome a disgraceful slowness and a dislike for work, and train your mind to think rapidly and to put forth strong efforts at the proper time. — SD 106.

Bewilderment Without God. The greatest minds if not guided by the word of God in their research, become bewildered in their attempts to trace the relations of science and revelation. — PP 113.

Effort. For the mind and the soul, as well as for the body, it is God's law that strength is acquired by effort. It is exercise that develops. In harmony with this law, God has provided in His word the means for mental and spiritual development. — Ed. 123.

Building on What We Have. Our intelligence will increase as we make use of that which we have. Our religious experience will strengthen as we bring it into the daily life. Thus we shall climb round after round of the ladder, reaching to heaven, until at last we step from off the topmost round into the kingdom of God. — 9T, 194.

A Vital Ratio. "...As in the case of Daniel, in exact proportion as the spiritual character is developed, the intellectual capabilities are increased. — SD 322 (R&H, Mar 22, 1898).

Balance in Reasoning. If the mind is set to the task of studying the Bible, the understanding will strengthen and the reasoning faculties will improve. Under the study of the Scriptures the mind expands and becomes more evenly balanced than if occupied in obtaining information from books that have no connection with the Bible. — CT 452.

Power of Simplicity. He who will observe simplicity in all his habits, restricting the appetite and controlling the passions, may preserve his mental powers strong, active, and vigorous, quick to perceive everything which demands thought or action, keen to discriminate between the holy and the unholy, and ready to engage in every enterprise for the glory of God and the benefit of humanity. — SD 86.

Misuse of the Mind. The mind does not wear out nor break down so often on account of diligent employment and hard study, as on account of eating improper food at improper times, and of careless inattention to the laws of health... Irregular hours for eating and sleeping sap the brain forces. The apostle Paul declares that he who would be successful in reaching a high standard of godliness must be temperate in all things. Eating, drinking, and dressing all have a direct bearing upon our spiritual advancement. — SD 172 [*CDF*]

The Whole Body. If the stomach is burdened with too much food, even of a simple character, the brain force is called to the aid of the digestive organs. There is a benumbed sensation upon the brain. It is almost impossible to keep the eyes open. The very truths which should be heard, understood, and practiced are entirely lost through indisposition, or because the brain is almost paralyzed in consequence of the amount of food eaten. — 2T 603.

Nature and the Mind. If the follower of Christ will believe His word and practice it, there is no science in the natural world that he will not be able to grasp and appreciate. There is nothing but that will furnish him means for imparting the truth to others. Natural science is a treasure house of knowledge from which every student in the school of Christ may draw. — COL 125

Total Transformation. By beholding we are to become changed; and as we meditate upon the perfections of the divine Model, we shall desire to become wholly transformed, and renewed in the image of His purity. It is by faith in the Son of God that transformation takes place in the character, and the child of wrath becomes the child of God. He passes from death unto life; he becomes spiritual and discerns spiritual things. The wisdom of God enlightens his mind, and he beholds wondrous things out of His law. As a man is converted by the truth, the work of transformation of character goes on. He has an increased measure of understanding. In becoming a man of obedience to God, he has the mind of Christ, and the will of God becomes his will.

He who places himself unreservedly under the guidance of the Spirit of God, will find that his mind expands and develops. — 1SM 338.

Warning: Danger of Being Very Bright. Satan will seek to draw you away from Christ, that you may become his agent in drawing others away, and thus frustrate the plans of God. He is the father of lies, and he weaves a net of falsehood in which he binds you with cords of lies to his service. The more intelligent you are, the more attractive, the harder he will work that he may persuade you to lay your talents at his feet, and aid him to accomplish his ends in alluring others under his black banner. If he can only keep the mind infatuated, he will do it. — SD 336.

Our Generous God. "If any of you lack wisdom, let him ask of God, that giveth to all men liberally, and upbraideth not, and it shall be given him. But let him ask in faith, nothing wavering. For he that wavereth is like a wave of the sea driven with the wind and tossed. For let not that man thing that he shall receive anything of the Lord." — James 1:5-7.

Experiment with Him to have real knowledge. Experience is knowledge derived from experiment. Experimental religion is what is needed now. "Taste and see that the Lord is good." 5T 221, 222.

Them that honor me
I will honor.
　　—I Sam 2:30

CHAPTER 13

NO HONOR LIKE BEING HONORED WITH GOD

Backdrop. *Everyone likes to be appreciated. But to see and hear our faith honored is something quite special, especially in areas where our religious, health, and educational beliefs and practices vary from conventional philosophies of the day.*

Not long ago I was invited as one of five living presidents of Nihon San-Iku Gakuin Daigaku [NSG or Japan Missionary College] who were honored on its 100th Anniversary. While there, a thoughtful staffer brought out a 50-year-old file of post-World War II letters of men and women who visited NSG during our tenure there when the College was operating a full-scale balanced program that we describe in Chapter 6 and 7, and which they still manage in our academies. Guests included preeminent educators, industrialists, statesmen and Prince and Princess Takamatsu. Their words illustrate the near reverence the Prince and great men held for EGW, her God, the book Education, and its influence on NSG's balance of teachers combining work with study. Here are a few...

First, the Prince's speech. From an American's point of view, this was much more than an honor. It revealed Japan's true national attitude toward royalty—something I knew little about. Dr. Erwin Syphers, head of our internationally-known Tokyo Sanitarium Hospital, invited me to accompany him to a reception by the International Student Association. When we found that Prince Takamatsu, an honored guest, was talking freely with conversational groups, we sidled over to one. The Prince quickly let us know that he knew our hospital well, and favorably.

He seemed excited about our college when we told him that our teachers worked manually with students on the campus, farm and in industries several hours each day to give them a mental and physical balance and to make them more employable and more thoughtful of blue collar workers. God answered our prayers when the Prince expressed an interest in witnessing such a program.

He wrote down in my little appointment book *Monday, May 6, 1952.* Dr. Yamagata translated for me as we announced the occasion to our student body in our Friday chapel, but at the close of that meeting he apologized to me for the behavior of the students.

"But why apologize, Sensei?" I was puzzled.

"They didn't believe you," he said. "They ridiculed you by their manners."

I had been in Japan less than a year, and was not acquainted with such quirks. He agreed to call the Prince's secretary and confirm the date. The gentleman understood our inexperience with royalty, and welcomed our offer of the EGW book, *Education.*

The next Monday at chapel Dr. Yamagata and I announced that the Prince's secretary had confirmed the appointment "For six weeks from today at 11 o'clock in the morning. And Princess Takamatsu will be with him." Then he added in good humor, "He is always prompt. You may set your watch by his arrival."

The students gasped. They hadn't believed that "the brother of `God' (the Emperor)" would ever come to a little school out in farm country 60 miles around Tokyo bay. And their awe was heightened when they learned that on that day police would be posted within sight of each other on the highways for the entire 60 miles, in touch with each other by phone. They said they would keep us informed!

But the students were not the only ones gasping. We too were gaining insights on great men and women such as God promised in Isaiah 54, 58 and 60, including royalty (60:10).

Dorothy asked me, "But Honey, we're vegetarians. What will I give them to eat?"

"Exactly the same as you feed me, "I replied. I'm a son of the *King* of kings. I spoke without hesitation, realizing later that the Holy Spirit must have given me those words. When Dorothy prepared breaded gluten cutlets made that day by the head of our health food industry, Sam Yoshimura (later known for Sam's Chicken from Worthington Foods), the Prince thought they were unusually-tender breaded veal cutlets, and asked for a second helping. We knew they would be delicious, but we also credited the Holy Spirit for influencing the royal taste that day.

While we were waiting for luncheon, the Prince sat on our living room divan with his arms around Dennis, 8, and Kathleen, 4, although part of the time she climbed up on his lap. He told them about his nephew, Crown Prince Akihito, then an early teenager who was taught at his mother's knee, and helped his father, Emperor Hirohito, in his famed botanical laboratory at the Imperial Palace.

After luncheon and a tour of our cherry- and pine-treed campus, the Prince stepped up to our new senior college inauguration podium and delivered these words, now inscribed as a foreword to the Japanese translation of the book *Education*:

"It is in a school like this...that a new life is brought into being. We hear that nature is the mirror of love, but man's spirit needs a constant training. And it is really a remarkable thing that here is...before us such a beautiful and unadulterated harmony of nature and man. True education is to learn of eternal wisdom...

"I have heard that in the history of Christianity, salvation through faith and love has led the hope of the world through the problem of sin. Now when...modern society is bringing fear, uncertainty and suffering, we are trying to overcome them and find the way by seeking salvation through faith....

"So, we must step forward by overcoming, when today we in the 20th Century are about to decide for eternal life or death, either light or darkness; and it is none other than education through love ...that will produce the joy for which we are looking. I believe that your school may be the place where this is to be...solved."

The Mizuno saga. Dr. Tsunekichi Mizuno, of Tamagawa University said he was compelled to insist that:

"EDUCATION, written with the inspired pen of Ellen G. White has for 50-some years been a well-known book which has rendered the greatest possible service and joy to students, teachers and parents the world over....We must, through Jesus Christ, the great Teacher sent by God, see the living God, Himself; must know His methods of teaching; and must attain to His eternal truth. Otherwise we cannot safely enjoy the name of a teacher in our schools....Nor shall we, needless to say, have the name of a teacher in the heavenly school of the future."

An eminent statesman. Kenjiro Matsumoto, elder statesman whose father was head of the Zaibatsu, Japan's industrial coalition before and during World War II, and founder of Kyushu Industrial University:

"My wife and I...extend our deepest appreciations...for the principles of education practiced at your institution, and were very much pleased by actually witnessing the operation of the three-fold education (as mentored by Ellen White)....

"Naturally, I have a deep interest in the ideal and practice of your institution with the hope that it will be an excellent example in the educational circles of Japan...."

A work-study scholar. An educator known simply as "Nagatoro", prefectural (state) board of education and university and private school association president, compared our program with his:

"Education in Japan today cannot produce real leaders to lead the New Japan, because the personal touch of the educator's love is not felt in it [like yours]. But here in this school students come under the personal guidance and influence of...capable teachers. Here is realized that which today's education in Japan comes short of. I earnestly desire that this school will stick close to this plan. This will be a remedy to the defect of education in Japan....

"Another point...its religious atmosphere. [Many talk] about bringing into education elements of spiritual, ethical, religious and

75

nature, but...lack religion that drives itself into the soul. ...I am firmly convinced that [your] teachers and students live such a life...."I... encourage you in behalf of Chiba Prefecture's private schools...to become the leaders of the New Japan with your great message...world view...love and religious conviction....After many, many years of experience...I feel an emotion when I look at young people with talents and glorious future."

Dr. Maurice Troyer. Vice-president for Curriculum and Instruction of International Christian University, Tokyo; former head of teacher education, Syracuse University, New York, and one of my teachers at University of Southern California:

"Your program in which students and faculty study, work and worship together is the only valid approach to education for Christian service. It breaks through the hierarchy of Japan's social structure in a meaningful way because it demonstrates the dignity of all kinds of work, and the value of each individual regardless of his kind of work. Your institution and our institution have much in common...."

A Preeminent industrialist. K. Ishibashi, head of Bridgestone Tire Co. Ltd. etc. and vehicle maker, the "Henry Ford of Japan," and his wife (Ishibashi means *Bridgestone),* tell of their visit to NSG:

"It was summer last year that my wife and I were invited to the anniversary ceremony of the inauguration of your college as a 4-year institution. The moment we entered your campus, we discovered...a most beautifully arranged school of the kind we would expect to see in some foreign land.

"The invisible strength of religious humility and industriousness that permeated the entire campus impressed us as being unique and struck us most powerfully during the whole course of the ceremony, and even more outstandingly, when we were shown around the campus.

"I could only but marvel at how you have put into practice the most essential, yet seldom-realized factor required in the current educational system of our country, namely the whole-hearted guidance of the soul and heart of your...superior leaders in not only teaching the truth of religion or...promoting industriousness, but in materializing this sacred spirit in every phase....the highest of cultural achievements...an example to contemporary youths of Japan...and the happiness of all mankind."

Veteran American Ambassador John M. Allison, who endeared himself to all American citizens in the Far East:

"Your objective of preparing youth for Christian service through training intended to bring the mental, physical, and spiritual powers of the individual into harmonious balance is a noble ideal—practical

training methods you have been using successfully. I speak as one who has also been strongly impressed over a period of years with the fine record of service to humanity made by your hospitals in the Far East."

Leading in the Philippines. God repeated his blessings at Philippine Union College (PUC-PI) where we were asked to strengthen an emerging masters degree program and start teacher participation in a work-study program. Although there was insufficient time to carry out as complete program, God helped us set up a reasonably balanced work/study program. But down in Bukidnon, a crew of Filipino and American leaders planned and established Mountain View College under the guidance of men like Reuben Manalaysay and a strong Filipino crew, Virgil Bartlett, Wilton Baldwin, William Richli, M.D., and by Don Christensen—who managed it for 17 years with all students and teachers working, and a record of 84% of the students working their way.

Dr. Daniel Salcedo, a Roman Catholic layman, head of private education, made his enthusiasm vividly known to the great President Ramon Magsaysay and the Philippine Congress. President Magsaysay then invited us to the Malacanan Palace. The Congressional delegation visited us to see the program in action, and the *Manila Times* banner-headlined eight PUC-Manila Sanitarium nurses out of the Philippine Nursing Board's top ten. We didn't seek such honors. God did it as He promised through Moses, Samuel and Ellen White: "Them that honor me, I will honor." [1Sam2:30] He delights to do this. [Deut 28; ED50] It was fun to test our Master.

Monaco. Nearly 25 years later God gave us quite a different experience. It wasn't with a school nor a government, but with another royal family, which caught the divine wisdom radiating from EGW. After *Reader's Digest* editors picked our article from the pages of the June,1972 *Harper's* Magazine, it sent 52,000,000 copies around the world, designating it as a "springboard for discussion" piece. It stirred the editors of Reader's Digest Press enough to ask for a book they named *Better Late Than Early,* whose research message cover to cover supported Ellen White. And that book reached at least one palace....

In 1976 we received a letter from the secretary of Princess Grace of Monaco expressing the Princess' interest in the book, and extending an invitation to talk with her if I were ever in the area. European travel was not in my yearly schedule, but God arranged a happy "coincidence." The International Academy of Preventive Medicine had asked for a talk on the "Dangers of early schooling" at Herdecke, Germany, a short day's travel from Monaco.

The Princess' secretary took me out to meet her in the garden. She was warm and informal in manner much like any gentle American woman. I wondered just what was on her mind. Before long I found that she was curious about our child development, learning and behavioral research. After half an hour or so, she became notably sober. During our conversation I did not think of media portrayals of her as a super star. It was just as well, for I had never seen her films. She had an inner loveliness that overrode her widely admired beauty. I knew of her deep devotion to children through the International Red Cross. But her mind was clearly on *her* children.

Then she paused, her throat convulsing slightly. With her eyes watering, she said, "Dr. Moore, if only I could do it over again, I would keep my children much closer to me. I would spend my time with them instead of The Red Cross." Not long afterward she was killed in an automobile accident, perhaps providentially spared the embarrassment of a greater tragedy international spotlight on her children who had to await a late, unchaperoned maturity. But I will never forget her words, "If only..."

I had seen Caroline, her oldest at 18, frolicking around a swimming pool nearby, and Stephanie, 12, racing up the circular stairway inside the Palace. There was no shocking behavior, but she seemed to have visions of what was to come with children whose family values had surrendered to their peers.

This was a sheer contrast of the conventional American system in which Grace was reared (in Philadelphia) and the Tokyo Imperial Palace. There, Prince Takamatsu told our children one day while waiting for lunch, how Emperor Akihito had learned at his mother's knee, and worked with his father, Emperor Hirohito, in his noted botanical laboratory. He was never allowed to lose sight— in language, thoughtfulness, manners, or integrity—that he was born to the palace. He is deeply loved and respected by his people Both families were reminders to us of many pages of EGW counsel and of Scripture in Romans 8:14-17 and Revelation 1:6, 5:10 and 3:21, KJV, and our invitation to sit with Christ on His *Eternal Throne*.

CHAPTER 14

THE GEORGE WASHINGTON OF NAPA TECH HIGH

Backdrop. *Ted and Becky Fujimoto were our hosts for a seminar in Napa, California. We admired their young children who were so outgoing, hospitable...and well behaved. They became especially interesting to us when we found that Ted had been working on developing a new, now famous, public high school in Napa. We found common ground in our highly successful homeschool formulas. This is not surprising, for both are inspired by the same source, Ellen White: Joint teacher-student work-study-service programs develop employable youth in public schools with teachers at their side, sharing work skills that warrant employability. This is much more important to God than shooting a basket or kicking or throwing a ball.*

It is not often that you meet a 30-year old whom state and federal leaders tout as a leading American educator. Yet that is exactly what we found in Napa: California Governor Pete Wilson hailed Ted as the designer of Napa's New Technology High School which Wilson called "California's model high school." He operates with substantial grants from corporations who are interested in his concepts of employability training. The influence of Ted's Learn City Corporation at this writing extends beyond America into Europe and the Western World.

High tech home boy. When she first saw New Tech after vacationing in Napa Valley for 30 years, JoAnne Miller, an eight-year president of the San Francisco School Board, was so astonished and pleased that she left her Bay Area job to become Tech's in-house consultant. She was thrilled by the success of a school so far from the typical mass-education machine, and totally bent on producing *high-character, creative, employable* youth. She wrote in the April 2000 *Converge Magazine*, "Is it any wonder that Mark Morrison, director of New Tech, and I look on Ted Fujimoto as our third arm, and that students who know him by sight refer to him as "New Tech's George Washington?"

Ted was homeschooled in the mission field and adjusted well to the idea of keeping their children at home. Yet Becky was one of seven day-care babies. Yet she wanted the best education for their children and took the time to visit many schools when Shannon became "school age." Her survey turned their curiosity into a decision to homeschool, despite family, church and peer pressures.

She pursued a work-study balance and the Moore formula that delays formal education until the child is ready, and then tailors the curriculum to each child's interests, aptitudes and abilities. Becky says that with God's help, they take one day at a time. They do very well.

We wouldn't have been so surprised when we first met Ted and Becky if we had known that we had so much in common.

Ted was homeschooled in the mission field, then entered California's Weimar Institute Academy's teacher-student work-study program; Pacific Union College.

He operates hand and heart in the kitchen with Becky, who is also his technological teammate and mother of two well behaved little Fujimotos, Shannon, 6 and Stephen, 4.

Ted's institutional experiences were at schools inspired by Ellen White.

After lecturing to a Northern California Conference seminar of Seventh-Day Adventist Academy principals, Ted was asked where he found such noteworthy sources for such highly technical ideas.

"Go to Ellen White," he replied, *and you will nail it down!"*

Mouths dropped and questions poured . Here are some of Ted's answers:
- Move ahead of [conventional] education reform... Go to the fundamental roots of Adventist education...adopt less of the classical education model.
- [There is now a] huge opportunity to increase enrollment with highly effective and focused education.
- Reduce costs of delivery by using "safe" courses online or through collaboration with other institutions.
- Take everything that EGW promotes and modernize it...[and] you have the cookbook to education reform.
- Parents are looking for alternatives...private education overall is going up...parents ARE willing to pay if they know what they are getting for their money.
- Don't try to duplicate everything. Algebra III could be taken online from an instructor with a great reputation from one of the leading universities. You will need to figure out what are the "safe" courses.
- Why teach Microsoft Office when you can get it online from a provider that has put $millions into the course development? Ted had caught the thrill and wonders of experimenting with God. [Deut. 28; PP290; ED50]

The forces of the Gentiles shall
come unto thee... They shall shew
forth the praises of the Lord.
—Isaiah 60:5,6

CHAPTER 15

ELLEN WHITE AND COLUMBIA UNIVERSITY'S BEST

Backdrop. *In February, 1958, several of us were standing in line for lunch at the Coffee Shop of the Hilton Hotel in Chicago. The occasion was a meeting of the American Association of Colleges for Teacher Education, for which I was then its in-house consultant at the National Education Association. Included in the "several" were Sam Wiggins, Dean of George Peabody College for Teachers, David Willis of Marquette University, W. H. Wood of Emmanuel Missionary College, and Florence Stratemeyer, professor of education in Teacher's College, Columbia University, New York City. Conversation turned to Ellen G. White's book 'Education.'*

"That is an amazing book." Dr. Stratemeyer exclaimed in her dignified, but forceful manner. "And to think that Mrs. White finished only three grades of school."

Then, turning to me, "You consider her a prophet, don't you?"

"We are very careful about whom we call a prophet," I returned, "but if we appraise her writings against the Bible standards for a prophet, we are compelled to believe she was."

Immediately the men about us were filled with questions. All were scholars and were surprised that they had not heard of the book before. All asked for the address of the publisher.

Sometime later that year, while visiting in her office, I noted *Education* lying on top of a number of manuscripts and asked her if she would mind talking to our Adventist teachers sometime about her impressions of this book. Later, she visited us at a study conference for Adventist educational supervisors, superintendents, and secretaries at Potomac University in Washington, D. C., (later moved to Michigan and renamed Andrews).

An Address Before Adventist Educators

In January, 1959, she stood before 70 leading Adventist educators in the Potomac University chapel. A tall, slender, silver-haired lady, she made a striking picture. On her right were her notes, complete as would be expected of so thorough a woman. On her left was her copy of *Education*, the topic to be

81

discussed. This copy had been given to her the year before by one of her Adventist doctoral students, Wesley Rhodes of Union College.

She constantly referred to her marked copy of *Education* as she discussed basic principles of education. She seemed to understand more than many Adventists the depth and import of this heaven-inspired book. Basing her thought on notes taken by a member of the conference, she declared:

"Democracy [and public education] respects one's rights as an individual; but here we see man created in the image and the likeness of God, a product of the Creator. You recognize free will and freedom of choice as basic values in a democracy. While democracy implies certain basic concepts, the values of a democratic society are subject to change in a changing world; but the values that you are trying to achieve are based on eternal verities, which you hold. They never change."

Dr. Stratemeyer (with graceful gesture) emphasized each point.

"If you follow your philosophy of education as outlined in this book," she continued, holding up *Education*, "you must teach a child to know why he acts as he acts. He must learn *how to think, how to reason,* for himself."

Turning to page 230 in *Education*, she read:

"The education that consists in the training of the memory, tending to discourage independent thought, has a moral bearing which is too little appreciated. As the student sacrifices the power to reason and judge for himself, he becomes incapable of discriminating between truth and error, and falls an easy prey to deception. He is easily led to follow tradition and custom. It is a fact widely ignored, though never without danger, that error rarely appears for what it really is."

As if to emphasize the ease with which we can be deceived, and more particularly the susceptibility of our children to deception, she turned to page 289.

"There is no question," she emphasized, "but that self-discipline is the best discipline. Just listen to this. 'The parent or teacher who by such instruction trains the child to self-control will be the most permanently successful.'"

Again and again Dr. Stratemeyer remarked on how remarkable it was that an unschooled woman could write as Mrs. White wrote. Back and forth she went between Mrs. White's writings and current educational developments, demonstrating in 1958 how Mrs. White was more than fifty years ahead of her time.

For example, one of the greatest of modern curriculum principles is that of concern for the "whole child." In other words, educators should think not only of his mind, but also of his physical, spiritual and social welfare. Mrs.White did not necessarily use current terminology," Dr. Stratemeyer pointed out. "In fact, she did not use the word *curriculum* in her writing. But the book *Education* in certain parts treats of important curriculum principles. She was concerned with

82

the whole learner." Dr. Stratemeyer emphasized the fact that Mrs. White held these advanced views *at the beginning of the last century.*

Education as the Harmonious Development of All Faculties

Here the distinguished woman turned to *Education*, page 13: "Education 'is the harmonious development of the physical, the mental, and the spiritual powers. It prepares the student for the joy of service in this world and for the higher joy of wider service in the world to come.' Here is beautifully stated one of the great curriculum principles—and in 1903!"

Continuing, she added:

"In contrast with emphasis on development of the intellect only, here we have the real education whose primary concern is with harmonious development. And here we have it in layman's language—concerned with the emotional, physical, intellectual, and spiritual. One can't think straight if he is ill physically.

"We, of course, must not neglect the intellect, for it is God's. It is the gift He has given to man over and above the beasts. Rather, we will strengthen it by a healthful balance."

Again and again the distinguished teacher referred to the importance of "the harmonious balance of the mental, physical, and spiritual powers." "If we had this balance," she pointed out, "we would act less on selfishness and more on principle. We would be setting a better example for our children to follow, by our own daily habits of rest, relaxation, sleep, exercise."

Dr. Stratemeyer's closing remarks summed up the whole goal of the study conference in the following words:

"My philosophy of education grows out of my philosophy of life. And this philosophy of life, with you as well as with me, will come from the tone of our spiritual lives. If you implement the basic concepts we have discussed, your educational leadership will be along positive, constructive lines."

In the Adventist Church all members are educators–officers, ministers, laymen, teachers. That is inescapable. The question that stung our complacency was, Are we following the plan that has been given us with the earnestness Dr. Stratemeyer, a preeminent curriculum authority, a Roman Catholic, expressed?

CHAPTER 16

ELLEN WHITE AND CORNELL'S WORLD-CLASS SCIENTIST*

Lecture given at the Unitarian Church, April 9, 1958*
By Clive M. McCay, Ph. D.
Professor of Nutrition, Cornell University, Ithaca, N.Y.

Backdrop in Dr. McCay's words. *For a quarter of a century the writer has taught a course for graduate students dealing with the history of foods and nutrition. In this course are presented original materials starting with the early Greek work by Athenaeus who lived in Rome at the end of the second century A.D. In the middle of the 13th century Petrus Hispanus published much about diet. Shortly after the discovery of America one of the greatest books about nutrition and old age was written by Luigi Cornaro. (1464-1566)*

Among writers of the past century, however, those who are concerned with the betterment of human health must pay tribute to the writings of Ellen G. White because she understood the importance of the selection of proper foods and the relation of the rest of the regime of living to proper nutrition and sound health. These notes have been prepared by a biochemist who specializes in nutrition in the hopes that others outside of the Adventists may gain a broader appreciation of the genius of this pioneer nutritionist, Ellen G. White. Whatever may be the religious belief of a reader, he or she cannot help but gain much guidance in a better and healthier way of life from reading the major works of Ellen G. White.

Every modern specialist in nutrition whose life is dedicated to human welfare must be impressed in four respects by the writings and leadership of Ellen G. White.

In the first place, her basic concepts about the relation between diet and health have been verified to an unusual degree by scientific advances of the past century.

In the second place, everyone who attempts to teach nutrition can hardly conceive of a leadership such as that of Mrs. White that was able to induce a substantial number of people to improve their diets.

In the third place, one can only speculate about many sufferers... who could have had improved health if they had accepted the teachings of Mrs. White.

Finally, one can wonder how to make her teachings more widely known in order to benefit the overcrowded earth that reams inevitable tomorrow unless the rate of increase of the world's population is decreased.

To appreciate the great need for dietary reform one can note the foods available to the average family during the first third of Mrs. White's lifetime starting in 1827 and ending with the outbreak of war between the states. The typical farm family, and most families lived on a farm, from Maine to Indiana had some chickens, swine, sheep and a few cows. A housewife looked after the garden and the chickens while the man labored in the field. The diet was reasonably satisfactory from the time rhubarb checked latent scurvy in April until most of the fresh foods had disappeared by Thanksgiving.

From Thanksgiving until Easter the diet grew progressively worse with outbreaks of disease in February and March. Although the French scientist, Appert, patented methods for canning food in 1810, the housewives had no containers for doing this until well after the Great War. Therefore, the housewife had to depend upon drying apples, sweet corn, peas and beans over her kitchen stove. Vinegar was available because the common fruit was apples. Salt was the other common preservative. Most meat was salted and smoked although pork was often fried and stored in earthenware jars with the meat sealed and sterilized by pouring hot lard over it. Pickles could be preserved and families of Germanic origin could make sour kraut.

Walnuts, hickory nuts and in some areas chestnuts were available. Salted fish were commonplace. Eggs were plentiful in summer and scarce in winter because there was no good way of preserving them except by storage in lime or sawdust.

Cellars preserved the potatoes and apples although the potatoes were often exhausted by spring and the family had to eat the seed and plant the peelings.

The Indiana children took corn bread for their lunch at school until well after the middle of the century. At home they had much corn meal mush and hominy. Highly refined white flour did not become common until after the middle of the century because the roller mills that could take out the germ and the vitamins from wheat flour were only invented about the middle of the nineteenth century.

Butter could be stored in crocks but was usually quite rancid when the cream was skimmed and became worse in storage.

Foods bought at the country stores usually consisted of salt fish or salt meat, some coffee or tea, some sugar and a jug of thick molasses. Since the molasses came north from New Orleans, the supply was cut off during the sixties and areas like Indiana developed a taste for the sour sorghum molasses.

In *Life Sketches* one learns much about both the bad food served in most homes and the toll of diseases that resulted. It is no wonder that the relationships between food and diseased people were deeply impressed upon the Whites as they traveled in New England and the Middle West more than a hundred years ago. The diet was a monotonous one of fat, salted meats, bread, potatoes and butter. No wonder that Elder White developed dyspepsia.

When foods were available, the Whites were plagued by poverty but kept their determination to remain free from debts. In 1847 Mrs. White wrote "I allowed myself and child one pint of milk each day. One morning before my husband went to work, he left me nine cents to buy milk for three mornings. It was a study with me whether to buy the milk for myself and babe or get an apron for him. I gave up the milk, and purchased the cloth to cover the bare arms of my child." (1T p. 83.)

Later in 1852 when the Whites lived in Rochester they had so little money that they could not afford potatoes and butter but ate turnips and sauce.

At this time meals at hotels cost twenty-five cents. Hard liquor was five cents extra. Plenty of men paid the extra although it is doubtful if the consumption of alcoholic beverages was equal to that of today since few women drank. Although cigarettes were not to become accepted until much later, there was much smoking and chewing of tobacco on the steamers and in the public waiting rooms.

The Whites in their travels must have often had the thought of Pascal that "Nothing more astonishes me than to see that men are not astonished at their own weakness."

Well before the birth of Mrs. White there were a few Americans reacting against the bad diet, the smoking and the drinking. Even from early antiquity there had been groups outside the Jewish traditions that subscribed to vegetarianism. In 1935 J. Haussleiter published a book of 427 pages dealing with vegetarianism in antiquity. Sylvester Graham who was born in 1794 stirred the young American nation with his lectures advocating vegetarianism, the improvement of bread, the abolishment of alcoholic beverages and more healthful living. He had much influence during the first half of the nineteenth century but left no permanent group of followers. The vegetarian church was founded in Philadelphia in 1817 but it languished and perished.

About 1840 the Shakers stopped the use of pork, strong drink and tobacco. Many turned to vegetarianism and Elder F. Evans of New Lebanon laid down rules of health which included:

1. Supply at least one kind of course grain bread per meal. Avoid cathartics.
2. Have the sickly and weakly cease using animal foods especially fats.
3. Keep the skin clean by regular bathing.

But the Shakers reached their peak about 1850 and have now almost perished.

Mrs. White must have long weighed the problems of health as she saw those around dying from cholera, typhoid fever, dysentery and tuberculosis. All of these have now been nearly eradicated by improved sanitation and better nutrition.

At the time of Mrs. White's birth, the chemists were beginning to establish the modern science of nutrition. Hundreds have now devoted their lives to creating this science. At this point it seems profitable to note a few of the teachings expressed in *The Ministry of Healing* and in *Counsels on Diet and Foods* in order to compare them with the accepted view points of modern nutritionists.

Today there is a widespread movement to reduce the intake of fats especially animal fats, in order to reduce the blood cholesterol and the dangers of atherosclerosis. Mrs. White wrote "Nut foods are coming largely into use to take the place of flesh meats... When properly prepared, olives, like nuts, supply the place of butter and flesh meats. The oil, as eaten in the olive, is far preferable to animal oil or fat." (*Ministry of Healing*, p. 298.)

Near the end of Mrs. White's life in 1915 men began to appreciate that the milling of white flour was removing most of the vitamins, part of the protein and the important trace minerals such as iron. Today nutritionists know that these vital constituents are lost when the bran and germ are taken from the wheat. Mrs. White wrote "For use in bread making the superfine white flour is not the best. Its use is neither healthful nor economical. Fine-flour bread is lacking in nutrition elements to be found in bread made from the whole wheat." (*Ministry of Healing,* p. 300)

In spite of her emphasis upon a given type of diet Mrs. White appreciated that there were some people who could not tolerate foods that were well suited to the majority. Today it is well recognized that there are a few people with very sensitive intestines that suffer if the diet has much fiber. Mrs. White wrote "Foods that are palatable and wholesome to one person may be distasteful, even harmful, to another." (*Ministry of Healing*, p. 320.) "Some cannot use milk, while others thrive on it.... For some the coarser grain preparations are good food, while others cannot use them." (*Ibid.*, p. 320.)

Today it is well recognized that overeating and overweight produce much ill health. This is one of the few areas in which all professional nutritionists agree. In face they give dull, public lectures on the subject *ad* nausea. Mrs. White wrote "There should not be a great variety at any one meal, for this encourages overeating and causes indigestion." (*Ibid.*, p. 299.) "Abstemiousness in diet is rewarded with mental and moral vigor... At each meal take only two or three kinds of simple food, and eat no more than is required to satisfy hunger." (*Ibid.*, pp. 308, 310.)

Today many people are restricting their use of salt in order to lower their blood pressure or in the hopes of preventing high blood pressure. Attempts are made to keep the sodium intake low by using baked products made with yeast instead of baking powder. Mrs. White wrote "Do not eat largely of salt." "The use of soda or baking-powder in bread making is harmful and unnecessary." (*Ibid.*, pp. 305, 300.)

Throughout the whole life of Mrs. White it was customary to eat elaborate meals upon the Sabbath. She wrote "We should not provide for the Sabbath a more liberal supply or a greater variety of food than for other days. Instead of this the food should be more simple, and less should be eaten in order that the mind may be clear and vigorous to comprehend spiritual things." (*Ibid.*, p. 307) All thinking people will agree with this today but some still fail to practice it.

Today we teach home economics throughout our whole nation. Mrs. White wrote "Cooking is no mean science, and it is one of the most essential in practical life. It is a science that all women should learn… To make food appetizing and at the same time simple and nourishing, requires skill." (*Ibid.*, pp. 302, 303)

Meals served in many courses have almost passed from the American home, due probably to the disappearance of maids rather than a comprehension of Mrs. White's philosophy "All food should be put on the table at once instead of courses so that one will know what is available and not overeat." (See *Ministry of Healing*, p. 306, 386)

A problem of much concern in America today is that children insist upon watching television and eating snacks in the late evening. They then arise too late in the morning to eat breakfast. Before noon they are tempted to eat snacks and thus spoil their lunch. Mrs. White wrote "Irregularities in eating destroy the healthful tone of the digestive organs, to the detriment of health and cheerfulness. And when the children come to the table, they do not relish wholesome food; their appetites crave that which is harmful to them." (*Ibid.*)

Every thinking person today would agree with some of the wise statements of Mrs. White such as "Pure air, sunlight, abstemiousness, rest, exercise, proper diet, the use of water, trust in divine power—these are the true remedies." (*Ibid.*, p. 127.) "Parents should early seek to interest their children in the study of physiology and should teach them its simpler principles… An education in the things that concern life and health is more important to them than a knowledge of many of the sciences taught in the schools." (*Ibid.*, pp. 385, 386.) "The best food for the infant is the food that nature provides. Of this it should not be needlessly deprived." (*Ibid.*, p. 383.) "In the entertainment of guests there should be greater simplicity." (*Ibid.*, p. 322.) "When wrong habits of diet have been indulged, there should be no delay in reform." (*Ibid.*, p. 308.)

"Take active exercise every day, and see if you do not receive benefit." (*Ibid.*, p. 310.) "One of the surest hindrances to the recovery of the sick is thentering of attention upon themselves." (*Ibid.*, p. 256.)

"There is a large class who will reject any reform movement, however reasonable, if it lays a restriction upon the appetite…. By this class, all who leave the beaten track of custom and advocate reform will be opposed, and accounted radical." (*Counsels on Diet and Foods*, p. 195.) Today this class is greatly strengthened in its opposition by the tremendous forces of advertising and the mass control of activities as described in such works as that of Vance Packard in Hidden Persuaders. Hence, improvement of the diet of people is probably far more difficult than it was in the time of Mrs. White.

Today most of us tolerate the smoke blown in our faces as we travel by air and we try to avoid getting holes burned in our clothing as we ride with cigarette smokers on hotel elevators. Today the press is filled with stories relating to smoking because they force increases in the advertising budgets of the tobacco companies, in order to attempt to offset the truthful disclosures. A recent article by Dr. D. G. Steyn in the South African publication, *Lantern*, states "Reference should be made to the possible relationship between smoking and coronary thrombosis." Mrs. White wrote "Tobacco is a slow, insidious, but most malignant poison.... It is all the more dangerous because its effects are slow and at first hardly perceptible." (*Ministry of Healing*, pp. 327, 328.)

In some respects it might be easier to write about the areas in which nutrition specialists and the writings of Mrs. White may seem to disagree because the area is much smaller. These areas are probably due to changes in food technology. The raw milk in the days of Mrs. White was a carrier for many contagious diseases such as tuberculosis, dysentery, and typhoid fever. She felt that cheese was not a satisfactory food. This may have been the result of observations that cheese was made under rather unsanitary conditions.

Products such as dry skim milk were unknown in the lifetime of Mrs. White. This area of technology has developed since her death. Today we realize that such milk is one of the best components of bread since it improves the quality of the cereal proteins. Mrs. White wrote "The use of milk [in bread] is an additional expense and it makes the bread much less wholesome." (*Ibid.*, p. 301.) Today we realize that the skim milk which was fed to the pigs in Mrs. White's time contains the most important nutrients of the milk in terms of calcium, protein and vitamins. This could not be known to Mrs. White since the beginning of the realization of the importance of milk as a source of calcium did not begin until about fifty years ago. Vitamins were not discovered until about the time of her death.

Mrs. White did recognize the importance of mixing a variety of grains. She stated "It requires thought and care to make good bread. But there is more religion in a good loaf of bread than many think." (*Counsels on Diet and Foods*, p. 316.) She recognized the truth from Ezekiel, "Take thou also unto thee wheat, and barley, and beans, and lentils, and millet, and fitches, and put them in one vessel, and make thee bread thereof." (Ezekiel 4:9.) Beans supplement the proteins of wheat bread as well as increase such essentials as calcium.

All stimulants and narcotics were opposed by Mrs. White. Were she alive today she would certainly be disturbed with the extensive and foolish use of modern tranquilizers.

In his book, *The Geography of Hunger*, Josue de Castro, has stressed the millions of people in the world that are suffering from malnutrition because of poor dietary practices. In parts of the world this is due to the few foods that are available. In our nation it is due to the great surplus and poor selection due to ignorance and the pressures of individual industries to force their products upon the public by subtle methods of advertising. The people of the world would serve themselves best if they produced part of their foods in their own gardens and if they followed a general plan of some wise leader such as Mrs. White.

Among nutritionists there is an acute awareness of the problem of feeding the ever-increasing population of the world. This has been well summarized recently in the Journal of the New York Academy of Sciences in an article by J. G. Harrar entitled "Food, Science and People." He notes the increase in the population of the earth from a half billion in the year 1700 to five times this number in 1950. It is hazardous to extrapolate into the future in regard to population growth because many developments are in the offing that may reverse the whole trend. Large numbers of chemicals are finding their way into the food supply in the form of additives, spray residues, drugs fed to poultry and meat animals as well as radioactive fallout materials such as strontium 90. Chemists are well on their way in developing compounds that will produce sterility when added to food supplies. There may be bacteria or viruses of unknown forms of disease on other plants to which the animals on earth have no resistance and one can conceive of the wiping out of the entire population of man and higher animals on earth.

These and many unanticipated events may check or destroy the human population. However, if this population grows at the present rate, basic changes are inevitable. When man feeds on animals such as a pig or a turkey upon the grains that he can eat, at least three fourths of the food value is lost. In other words four men can live upon plant foods directly in comparison with the one man that can be fed if the food is first converted into meat and then consumed by man. Mrs. White stated this "The life that was in the grains and vegetables passes into the eater. We receive it by eating the flesh of the animal. How much better to get it direct, by eating the food that God provided for our use." (*Ministry of Healing*, p. 313.)

Man cannot eat much grass and hay so the cow serves us in changing this to milk. However, the chemists are busy taking such products out of hay as the protein so it can be eaten by man. Methods are being devised to break down the cellulose in plants so it can be digested by man. Each day in Wisconsin are made many tons of yeast from the wastes of paper mills. Yeasts are among the simpler plants that are readily digested by man. Yeasts are among the richest foods in vitamins and protein. In other words, many already know how to convert wood into human food. He can do the same for hay or straw because these can also be made into yeast.

As the population of the earth gets very large, most people will have to turn largely to vegetarian diets. Furthermore, as the demand increases for grains for cereal foods, man will no longer be able to afford the luxury of alcoholic beverages. At present grains are fermented and the alcohol is distilled off. The valuable food residues of vitamins, protein and minerals are now fed to animals to produce meat, milk and eggs. In order to feed large populations, alcohol production will have to cease since it involves the use of grains that can be eaten by man.

Likewise, as food becomes scarce man will no longer be able to afford the luxury of wasting land in the production of tobacco. Usually this is rich land for growing grains.

These changes to universal vegetarianism, is the cessation of making alcohol and the growing of tobacco will not occur within our lifetime but certainly may be expected within a century unless vast numbers of people are killed or the growth of the population is checked.

At present our problem is to discipline ourselves in our food habits and ways of living in order to insure the best possible health. In spite of the fact that the works of Mrs. White were written long before the advent of modern scientific nutrition, no better overall guide is available today. The great need is for people to read fewer books and to devote their efforts to the good ones.

You are writing each day a letter to all;
Take care that the writing is true.
Its the only gospel some people may read,
The gospel according to you.

-Author unknown

Let it not be that outward adorning...
but let it be the ornament of
a meek and quiet spirit...
in the sight of God of great price.
—1 Peter 3:3,4

CHAPTER 17

DRESSING TO MEET THE KING OF KINGS

Backdrop. *Please, before you read this chapter, stop and think of what your lifestyle will be when God permits you to go through "the time of Jacob's trouble and be translated when "faces are turned to paleness," as described in Jeremiah 30:5-7 and Great Controversy 616. "Before the final visitation of God's judgments upon the earth, there will be, among the people of the Lord, such a revival of primitive godliness as has not been witnessed since apostolic times." [GC 464] Are you, am I, ready to meet the King of kings who requires us to be so stripped of the world before He clothes us with heaven, a truly primitive godliness?*

We debated before including this chapter in this book, initiated primarily on research relating to education instructions from Scripture and Ellen White. Yet those who know us well, believe that the stories here told are as significant in upholding truths of God as findings of sound research. When you read this chapter, please be patient and read it in context, for we are dealing with eternal values that sometimes elude us in a society devoted to conventional wisdom and practice—so much so that some of the suggestions here may seem eons out of style, and certainly unpopular in some quarters. Yet, before you finish this chapter, you will read one of the best all-round descriptions of Christian dress that hold to standards laid down all through the EGW writings. And you will be surprised at who carried it out.

In his *Inside Report*, "How Much Is Too Much?" Doug Batchelor has some strong ideas, logically stated: "I have never heard a man say, "Isn't she beautiful? Just look at her jewelry!" We are not talking here about simple wedding rings, although some lavish archetypes may qualify. We do our best to simply face cultural trends which in fact are pagan by initiation, and lay on the line some significant ways to influence youth and adults for the Kingdom and make ready a generation of youngsters who have a sense of being born to the palace of when they sit down with Jesus on His throne where gold is transparent, and jewels are eternal. [Rev 3:21]

We do wonder if those who buy into present trends toward decorating their bodies with eye, mouth and body paint and tattoos, and with metal barbs and hangings, may have overlooked their examples to their children or to weak or prospective members and colleagues in the Church. Are they serious about soon entering a city whose walls are made of jewels that would make our treasures look like paste, and whose streets are paved with transparent gold that would make ours seem like dust?

What are your kids really thinking? A surprise for parents. Few moms and dads really have any idea of the inner thoughts of their children. The results of our studies of their inward preferences are unbelievable to most parents. So before we tell them of the results of our research which we usually had just done with *their* children, we challenge them to guess the answers. The replicability of our studies on youthful thought is the best test of our research. In more than 50 replications over the last 20 years, the results have always been consistent. Understanding them is crucial to family readiness for evangelism. And helps in preparing youth to accept God's messenger, Ellen White.

To do this, we hand a simple questionnaire to each member of any youth group in the critical transitional age range between childhood and adulthood: 11 to 15. The brief questionnaire asks, "If you have only two choices out of the following six, which would you choose? *Mark A for your first choice and B for your second.*" Then we list the following, although not necessarily in this order: *1. To get along well with your agemates? 2. To have a good relationship with your parents and their hopes for you? 3. To graduate well? 4. To be happily married? 5. To be rich and have a Corvette? 6. To be saved? (or have eternal life?).* We caution verbally, "Please keep your ballot entirely to yourself." When we are through, we have the youngsters total the figures. In a separate meeting we ask parental groups to guess the answers. Most guess **#1** or **#5**. Yet correct answers are always **6** and **2**. During ages **15** to **19,** the correct answers are **6** and **2** or **4.**

Principled thinking. So let's pass on some EGW principles in a day when our youth avidly copy adult trends from what we eat and drink to what we wear, how we travel and how we spend our spare time. For example, would your eligible son prospect for a wife who is adorned by an earth-bound goldsmith or would he follow Peter's and Paul's counsel and search for one who is adorned *within,* aware that God's design crew has jewels awaiting her entrance to heaven?

If jewelry is more likely to become an idol for women, we men must be careful about pointing fingers. We have our idols, too. For many it is cars, pickups or sport utility vehicles. Each must decide for himself whether he is buying a car for its special wheels and leather trim, or because it has the best running gear, economy or resale. It's not my business to judge you. Furthermore, God through EGW allowed that while wedding rings are "unnecessary," He did not give her firm negatives on them. Rather, He chose positives: First in giving us His *whys*: They tend to glorify self, are in most cases not really needed, our money is better spent on His work, and He is planning something much better for us!

For me, even gifts can feed my idolatry. I am a car buff. About 20 years ago our SDA Board chairman who also chaired a major division of Ford Motor Company, offered us a Lincoln sedan for the price of a Ford. It was tempting. Yet at the time, because of a story that was making the rounds, we felt that we had to refuse his offer: A friend on a year's furlough from the Far East was given a large, nearly new Cadillac that raised eyebrows at the churches he visited. On the other hand one of our board members later gave our Foundation money for a car, insisting that it must be big enough to be safe for Dorothy. So we disposed of our old car just short of 90,000 miles (where resale prices seem to change abruptly) and bought a used mid-size model with a good safety record and only 40,000 miles, for less than a new smaller car.

Idols vs. needs. That raises another question: What is the difference between an idol and a need? Do we think to principle—get down to basic *whys*—or are we prisoners of convention? Here EGW always makes common sense. Are we personally adorning self, and operating institutions along Heaven's guidelines? or do we operate from the world's viewpoint? I learned an unexpected lesson in 1976 while on a speaking trip in Europe, traveling on a Eurail Pass from Munich to Copenhagen via Hamburg. Just before we left, a beautiful young woman with a lovely 13-year-old girl boarded the train and sat opposite me in our two-seat, six-passenger compartment. They toted only a Haselblad camera, matching photographic equipment and their lunch. Neither wore any cosmetics nor jewelry.

I assumed correctly that they were photographer and model, out for the day. But I didn't learn until later that they were mother and daughter—Mrs. Mueller and Heidi—for neither wore a ring. When I told her that European friends in Washington, D.C. had said that wedding rings were essential in Europe, and had started a trend in our Church in America, she said, "It's just a matter of the mind." They invited me on my return to stay overnight with them at Interlachen, Switzerland where I found that Mr. Mueller descended from an eminent European theologian, and was one of Europe's master goldsmiths. I watched him fire gold to a liquid state as he fashioned a coat-of-arms for one of Europe's royal families.

When changing trains at Hamburg for Copenhagen, a middle-aged, richly-dressed woman occupied one of the two wide seats in the compartment to which I was assigned. I noticed that she had no wedding band, so assumed she was unmarried, until she told me that her husband owned a chain of pharmacies on the French Riviera. When I repeated my story from European friends in

Washington that wedding rings were mandated in Europe, she said, "Not at all. It may be conventional, yet we do whatever we want."

Dorothy and I never feel critical of anyone who wears a wedding ring, although I never do ring ceremonies when performing marriage rites. We don't make judgments, although we do let them know what God says through His messenger. Some women tell us that they wear wedding rings as a "a protection." Yet men are quick to advise otherwise. During World War II, soldiers and officers were not shy about pointing out that for a momentary liaison, they would rather "chance" a woman with a wedding ring than risk an unmarried woman. Married women, they felt, would more likely "know the risks."

Over a 100 years ago Ellen White made clear her messages from Heaven about jewelry. One story she told was about a new Adventist lady who had been rightly taught on the basis of *1 Timothy 2:9* and *1 Peter 3:3* "that Seventh-day Adventists did not wear jewelry, gold, silver or precious stones, and that they did not conform to worldly fashions in their dress." [EV270-71] After staying several weeks at one of our institutions, the lady was "bewildered." When, after baptism, she took off her jewels, one of the Adventist employees urged her to put them back on. "We are not so particular as formerly," the attendant said. "Our people have been over scrupulous in their opinions on the subject of dress. The ladies of this institution...dress like other people." To this, EGW declared,

> God's word is plain. Its teachings cannot be mistaken. Shall we obey it, just as He has given it to us, or shall we seek to find how far we can digress and yet be saved?... Conformity to the world is a sin which is sapping the spirituality of our people, and seriously interfering with their usefulness....We are nearing the close of this world's history....No one precise style has been given me as the exact rule to guide all in their dress....[EV273]

Then she said God calls for implicity, modesty, plain, durable material, "appropriate for this age."

We quote her exactly on wedding rings, for she has often been misquoted. She says in *Testimonies to Ministers* page 180-81, "Not one penny should be spent for a circlet of gold to testify that we are married." Then she adds a guarded exception:

> "In those countries where the custom is imperative," we have no burden to condemn those who have their marriage ring; let them wear it if they can do so conscientiously; but let not our missionaries feel that the wearing of the ring will increase their influence one jot or tittle. If they are Christians, it will be manifest in their Christlikeness of character... words...works...home... association with others... patience...kindliness."

Note her condition, "In those countries where the custom is imperative."

That is a tempting caveat to some, yet the two ladies from Switzerland and the Riviera gave us something to think about.

During our lifetime, the remarkable changes Dorothy and I have seen in personal dress, adornment and behavior have been almost as astonishing as has technology. The standard radio in the early 1920's was a crystal set, and the California State speed limit when we received our auto licenses at age 14, was 25 miles per hour. We plowed with mules and milked by hand. But styles have also changed dramatically. A woman who painted and plucked around her eyes was assumed to be an actress of questionable morals or a harlot, or was related to Jezebel or Aholah and Aholibah. [2Kings9:30, Jer4:30, Eze23:40-45] Obviously-painted lips were never seen in church. And even a gold watch marked you as pretentious, prodigal or an heir to wealth. Men's ties varied from narrow to wide and back again, and again; skirts went up and down from near the hips to close to the ankles, and back up. But through all of this and many times more, God's messenger spoke steadily of the principle of modesty and avoiding excitement of lusts of the other gender. Now how important is paint and style? Not very....

When we were first invited on the television circuit in the early 1970s, we were guests of studio *green rooms* and makeup chairs. But we soon found that more time, money and cosmetics were spent for religious shows than for secular. This is still in full swing on big interdenominational shows. Although their directors say it is a matter of photographic quality, we don't find that a concern of major networks; they spend little time or money these days on makeup. It became clear that mature operations which we shared—TODAY, OPRAH et al— didn't equate paint and powder with quality. The cover of the November 1999 *Reader's Digest* confirms this in their photo of preeminent actress Merle Streep who appears almost totally void of cosmetics. Even her inconspicuous blonde eyebrows seem without accentuation.

Ellen White used the words "cosmetics" and "artificials" as synonyms. In both cases, she notes that good health makes them unnecessary. [MLT143,CG424] She also observes that "The pure religion of Jesus requires of its followers the simplicity of natural beauty and the polish of natural refinement and elevated purity, rather than the artificial and false." Great artists and photographers are keenly aware of how a slight touch of mascara or shading on the eyes can create a question of character behind those eyes. Scripture suggests that the eyes are the windows of the soul. [Job19:27; Ps25:15,121:1; Isa6:5; Matt6:22, 20:15]: Noble examples by parents are wondrous lessons for youth. *Any meddling with the eyes reduces their influence, lessens their power.*

Overdecked men and women, cluttered with distractive adornments, must overwork to impress others that they are real, that they are mature. Such intrusion is a primrose path to *self-esteem*, but not the high road to *self worth*. Whatever your disposition, you won't find extreme solutions from Ellen White in this matter of outward distractions. All through her books, she simply and beautifully tells of God's logical and sure way to prepare for the kingdom which we welcome very soon. And speaking of this road to self worth, we adapt *This Week* Magazine's surprising example for *all* youth. Jhan and June Robbins explain clearly the kind of secular models that in some respects out-do us in achieving the EGW goals, principles and methods we try to define in this book:

Students in a Buffalo high school installed a full-length, plate-glass mirror at one end of a heavily traveled corridor. Over it they hung a sign: "Look! This is you. Are you satisfied?"

At first there were few positive answers, but soon it was mostly "Yes." The idea became contagious in the City schools. Boys and girls adopted "dress right" regulations which, teachers say, cut classroom horseplay 50 per cent, produced an astonishing change for the better in student attitudes, and gave the kids a sense of self worth.

They became really proud of how nice they looked. To see how appearance-conscious the students actually were, *This Week* Magazine set up a two-way mirror, provided by Libbey-Owens Ford Glass Company, in one high school, and stationed a photographer behind it, unseen by those who were photographed as they passed by. Students not only stopped to look at their reflections in the glass, they also stopped to "spruce up."

It wasn't always this way. Buffalo's school-age youngsters once delighted in dressing with calculated slovenliness. Sweat shirts, sneakers or boots, and soiled, ragged jeans made up the usual boys' costume. Girls hobbled themselves in tightly-fitted, pencil-slim skirts or, in warm weather, appeared in Bermuda shorts. Sweaters that seemed to have shrunk alarmingly were the usual toppers. One day Superintendent of Schools Joseph Manch stood up in a high-school auditorium and surveyed the assembled student body with a feeling of profound shock.

School or Clambake? "As far as I could see there wasn't a single tie, buttoned collar or ironed shirt in the school," he told us. "Some of the girls looked as though they were auditioning for a night-club chorus--others like female stable hands. Parents and teachers alike were complaining of poor discipline in the classrooms, uproar on school buses, disrespect for teachers and disinterest in learning. What occurred to me was this: If we let our students show up for class dressed for a hay ride or a clambake, can we really blame them if they act as if they're on one?

Buffalo's 14 high schools have a city-wide Inter-High School Student Council. Dr. Manch handed the problem to this group. The time had come, he said firmly, to do something about the way students dress. To his surprise, the council agreed. They decided to draw up a voluntary "dress right" code and went to work on it.

97

Dr. Manch observed, "It was almost as if they were relieved to have someone take a strong stand. They were ready to clean up, but nobody wanted to do it alone."

Within the month, the code was completed. The new rules were read at assemblies, posted on bulletin boards, sent home in mimeographed leaflets to parents. It took about half a term to get general compliance.

The program took hold in a good-natured atmosphere. In one high school, boys who appear in the morning without neckties are sent to the "Breakfast Club" (the principal's office) to rent ties, the biggest and gaudiest imaginable, for two cents a day. In another school, a history teacher keeps a supply of ties on hand for offenders and puts them on the kids himself, making sure they are tied as peculiarly as possible.

At the start, some parents had to go out and buy their children proper school clothes. Authorities expected some protests on this score but received very few. One parent did telephone her child's teacher to say it was entirely too much trouble to dress her son every day as if he were going to Sunday school. The teacher replied that the new dress code was concerned with neatness and did not require elaborate, expensive clothes.

Clothes Influence Behavior. At the end of the first year, parents and children were so completely sold that PTA groups in the city's elementary schools voted their own dress-right code into effect. Meanwhile, educators across the country were taking note. Many agreed that there is a startling association between unkempt, bizarre school clothing and rebellious, antisocial behavior. A Chicago high school principal told the National Education Association that two-thirds of all students brought to his office as disciplinary cases were dressed as rough-necks.

A public school principal in Cleveland told us, "There's no doubt that a great many of our youngsters turn in inferior academic performances because there are not enough visible signposts to show them where fun stops and work begins."

Our current free-and-easy attitudes toward school clothing are fairly recent. In the 1920's and 30's, many of our big city public schools had quite severe standards. Girls were told to wear long-sleeved white blouses and dark pleated skirts. Boys were ordered to appear in an ironed shirt, tie and dark wool pants. The rule served a three-fold purpose. There was no economic competition over who owned the flashiest clothes or the biggest wardrobe. There were no distractions of the tight-sweater variety. Most important, it was clearly a no-nonsense costume.

Educators now concerned with "dress right" programs are not generally in favor of a return to this unimaginative kind of uniform. They point out, however, that the blue-jeans crowd has established its own uniform. At an age when everyone wants to be one of the crowd, it's a tough job persuading students to dare to look different.

"You can't legislate 'dress right' rules," Dr. Manch said. "The beauty of our program is that it is voluntary."

For the guidance of interested student and parent groups, here are the recommendations made by Buffalo's student council committee:

Recommended for Boys: 1. Dress shirt and tie or conservative sports shirt and tie with suit jacket, sport coat or sweater. 2. Standard trousers or khakis, clean and pressed. 3. Shoes, clean and polished; white bucks acceptable (Not recommended are dungarees or soiled, unpressed khakis; T-shirts, sweat shirts; extreme styles of shoes including hobnail or motorcycle boots).

Recommended for Girls: 1. Blouses, sweaters, blouse and sweater, jacket with blouse or sweater. 2. Skirts, jumpers, suits or conservative dresses. 3. Shoes appropriate to the rest of the costume (Not recommended are V-neck sweaters without blouses; Bermuda shorts, party-type dresses, slacks; ornate jewelry; T-shirts, sweat shirts).

This is not, of course, the only acceptable program. But one thing is sure. This is one needed school reform that is cheap, quick and surprisingly easy. Buffalo's Dr. Joseph Manch is no longer superintendent 40 years later, but his legacy lives on. And the results, as Buffalo and other American cities learned, are astonishingly good.

And best of all, such students are more mature, creative, poised, and excited with a sense of what it means to be born to the palace.

An adaption of an article from *This Week* Magazine, November 23, 1958, by Jhan and June Robbins*.

TOUCHING THE FACE OF GOD

Oh, I have slipped the surly bonds of earth
And danced the sides on laughter-silvered wings,
Sunward I've climbed and joined the tumbling mirth
Of sun-split clouds—and done a hundred things
You have not dreamed of—wheeled and soared and swung
High in the sunlit silence. Hov'ring there
I've chased the shouting wind along and flung
My eager craft through footless halls of air
Up, up and long delirious, burning blue
I've topped the windswept heights with easy grace
Where never lark, or even eagle flew.
And, while with silent, listing mind I've trod
The high untrespassed sanctity of space,
Put out my hand, and touched the face of God.

American Lieutenant John Magee, who joined the Canadian Air Force as a volunteer in 1940 and was killed in action over England a year and a half later. He was 19. His only poem. Thousands of Canadians have memorized its 14 glorious lines and millions of Americans should. -- E.A Solis

Christ should be in [students'] hearts...
Refreshing all with whom they come in contact.
—6T 172-3; (MYP 406)

CHAPTER 18

SOCIAL CONDUCT
FOR THOSE WHO ARE BORN TO THE PALACE
By Ellen G. White

Backdrop. *This is an abridged compilation of quotations we prepared for the students and faculty of Pacific Union College by the Student Personnel Service, with the encouragement of the Executive Council of the Associated Students, and of the Student Personnel Committee of the College. These principles and practices are now being renewed in a large movement in many evangelical homes and schools. We have found that a sound, consistent teacher-student work-study-service program is the only truly happy way to embrace the standards here...*

GENERAL

Christian sociability is altogether too little cultivated by God's people. This branch of education should not be neglected in our schools. Students should be taught that they are not independent atoms, but that each one is a thread which is to unite with other threads in composing a fabric. In no department can this instruction be more effectively given than in the school homes where students are daily surrounded by opportunities which if improved will greatly aid in developing social traits of their character. It lies in their own power so to improve their time and opportunities so as to develop a character that will make them happy and useful. MYP 405

Soul Winners. Specially should those who have tasted the love of Christ develop their social powers for in this way they may win souls to the Savior. 4T 172 See also 4T 432.

Peer Dependence. The dangers of the young are greatly increased as they are thrown into the society of a large number of their own age, of varied character and habits of life. CT 332

Eternal Values Audited. One earnest, conscientious, faithful young man in a school is an ever inestimable treasure. Angels of heaven look lovingly upon him, and in the ledger of heaven is recorded every work of righteousness, every temptation resisted, every evil overcome. He is laying up a good foundation against the time to come, that he may lay hold on eternal life. CT 98-9

There is not one youth in one hundred who feels his God-given responsibility. (They) will be called to strict account. 5T 115

FRIENDSHIP

True Love. The warmth of true friendship, the love that binds heart to heart, is a foretaste of the joys of heaven. MH 360

Let all who would form a right character choose associates who are of a serious, thoughtful turn of mind and who are religiously inclined. If you turn from good counsel and choose to associate with those who you have reason to suspect are not religiously inclined, although they profess to be Christians, you will soon become like them. 4T 587-589

COURTSHIP

Infatuation. The young are in danger; but they are blind to discern the tendencies and result of the course they are pursuing. Many of them are engaged in flirtation. They seem to be infatuated. There is nothing noble, dignified, or sacred in these attachments; as they are prompted by Satan, the influence is such as to please him. Warnings to these persons fall unheeded. They are headstrong, self-willed, and defiant. They think the warning, counsel, or reproof does not apply to them. Their course gives them no concern. They are continually separating themselves from the light and love of God. They lose all discernment of sacred and eternal things; and while they may keep up a dry form of Christian duties, they have no heart in these religious exercises. All too late, those deceived souls will learn that strait is the gate, and narrow is the way, which leadeth unto life, and few there be that find it. 4T 589

The young affections should be restrained until the period arrives when sufficient age and experience will make it honorable and save to unfetter them. Those who will not be restrained will be in danger of dragging out an unhappy existence. A youth not out of his teens is a poor judge of the fitness of a person as young as himself to be his companion for life. MYP 452

Willfulness. Satan controls the minds of the youth in general. Your daughters are not taught self-denial and self-control. They are petted, and their pride is fostered. They are allowed to have their own way, until they become headstrong and self-willed, and you are put to your wits end to know what course to pursue to save them from ruin. Satan is leading them on to be a proverb in the mouth of unbelievers, because of their boldness, their lack of reserve and womanly modesty. The young boys are likewise left to have their own way. They have scarcely entered their teens before they are by the side of little girls of their own age, accompanying them home and making love to them. 2T 460

Impulsiveness. The youth trust altogether too much to impulse. They should not give themselves away too easily, nor be captivated too readily by the winning exterior of the lover. Courtship as carried on in this age, is a scheme of deception and hypocrisy, with which the enemy of souls has far more to do than the Lord. Good common sense is needed here if anywhere; but the fact is, it has little to do in the matter. FE 105

Mental Handicaps. Under the debasing power of sensual indulgence, or the untimely excitement of courtship and marriage, many students fail to reach that height of mental development which they might otherwise have attained CT 88

PURPOSE OF COLLEGE REGULATIONS: ACCOUNTABILITY OF TEACHERS

Common Dangers. One of the great objects to be secured in the establishment of the College was the separation of our youth from the spirit and influence of the world, from its customs, its follies, and its idolatry. The College was to build a barrier against the immorality of the present age, which makes the world as corrupt as in the days of Noah. The young are bewitched with the mania for courtship and marriage. Lovesick sentimentalism prevails. Great vigilance and tact are needed to guard the youth from these wrong influences. 5T 60

Accountability. I told the principal and teachers that God had laid upon them the responsibility of watching for souls as they that must give account. I showed them that the wrong course pursued by some of the students would mislead other students, if it were continued, and for this God would hold the teachers responsible. Some students would attend school who had not been disciplined at home, and whose ideas of proper education and its value were perverted. If those were allowed to carry things in their way, the object for which the school was established would be defeated, and the sin would be charged against the guardians of the schools, as if they had committed it themselves. CT 102

Faith or Fear? Some may urge that if religious teaching is to be made prominent, our school will become unpopular; that those who are not of our faith will not patronize the college. Very well, then let them go to other colleges, where they will find a system of education that suits their taste

Firm Standards. If a worldly influence is to bear sway in our school, then sell it out to worldlings, and let them take the entire control; and those who have invested their means in that institution will establish another school, to be conducted not upon the plan of popular schools nor according to the desires of principal and teachers, but upon the play which God has specified. CT 88

Love or Sickness? The youth whose influence is demoralizing should have no connection with our college. Those who are possessed of a lovesick sentimentalism, and make their attendance at school an opportunity for courting and exchanging improper attentions, should be brought under the closest restrictions. Authority must be maintained. Justice and mercy are twin sisters, standing side by side. 4T 209

Reverence or Degradation? Nothing can more effectually prevent or banish serious impressions and good desires than associations with vain, careless, and corrupt-minded persons. Whatever attractions such person may possess by their wit, sarcasm, and fun, the fact that they treat religion with levity and indifference is sufficient reason why they should not be associated with. The more engaging they are in other respects, the more should their influence be dreaded as companions, because they throw around an irreligious life so many dangerous attractions. 3T 125

The matter of choosing associates is one which students should learn to consider seriously. Among the youth who attend our schools there will always be found two classes, those who seek to please God and to obey their teachers, and those who are filled with a spirit of lawlessness. CT 221 See also 3T 24

God's Standards vs. Man's. We have labored hard to keep in check everything in the school like favoritism, attachments, and courting. We have told the students that we would not allow the first thread of this to be interwoven with their schoolwork. On this point we are as firm as a rock. I told them they must dismiss all ideas of forming attachments while at school. The young ladies must keep themselves to themselves, and the young gentlemen must do the same. *E.G. White, in Taylors Outline Studies, Appendix. Note 8*

Blind Love. Some of those who attend the College...rebel against the rules that will not allow young gentlemen to pay their attentions to young ladies. Full well is known the evil of such a course in this degenerate age. In a college where so many youth are associated...The infatuations on the part of both young men and women in thus placing the affections upon each other during school days, shows a lack of good judgment....blind impulse controls reason and judgment. Under this bewitching delusion the momentous responsibility felt by every sincere Christian is laid aside, spirituality dies, and the judgment and eternity lose their awful significance... Every faculty of those who become affected by this contagious disease *blind love* is brought in subjection to it. With many the crisis of the disease is reached in an immature marriage, and when the novelty is past, and the bewitching power of love-making is over, one or both parties awake to their true situation. They then find themselves ill-mated, but united for life. 5T 110

Toward Nobility. The wild, reckless character of many of the youth in this age of the world is heart sickening. If the youth could see that in complying with the laws and regulations of our institutions, they are only doing that which will improve their standing in society, elevate the character, ennoble the mind, and increase their happiness, they would not rebel against just rules and wholesome requirements, nor engage in creating suspicion and prejudice against these institutions. CT 99, 100

In our schools in Battle Creek, Healdsburg, and Corranbong, I have borne a straight testimony concerning these matters. There were those who thought the restraint too severe; but we told them plainly what could be and what could not be, showing them that our schools are established at great expense for a definite purpose, and that all which would hinder the accomplishment of this purpose must be put away... I told them that if they did not keep themselves to themselves, and endeavor to make the most of their time, the school would not benefit them, and those who were paying their expenses would be disappointed. I told them that if they were determined to have their own will and their own way, it would be better for them to return to their homes and to the guardianship of their parents. This they could do at any time, if they decided not to stand under the yoke of obedience; for we did not design to have a few leading spirits in wrong doing demoralizing the other students. CT 101, 102 See also 4T 433

Escorting. The rules of this college (an outside school) strictly guard the association of young men and young women during the school term. It is only when these rules are temporarily suspended, as is sometimes the case, that gentlemen are permitted to accompany ladies to and from public gatherings. Our own College at Battle Creek has similar regulations, though not so stringent. Such rules are indispensable to guard the youth from the danger of premature courtship and unwise marriage. Young people are sent to school by their parents to obtain an education, not to flirt with the opposite sex. FE 62 See also CT 100

SPECIAL PRIVILEGES TO MATURE STUDENTS

In all our dealings with students, age and character must be taken into account. We cannot treat the young and the old just alike. There are circumstances under which men and women of sound experience and good standing may be granted some privileges not given to the younger students. The age, the conditions, and the turn of mind must be taken into consideration. We must not lessen our firmness and vigilance in dealing with students of all ages, nor our strictness in forbidding the unprofitable and unwise association of young and immature students. CT 101

The older students in our schools should remember that it is in their power to mold the habits and practices of the younger students; and they should seek to make the best of every opportunity. Let those students determine that they will not through their influence betray their companions into the hands of the enemy. CT 225

CONVERSATION

For Angel Ears? Girls and boys get together, and chat, and laugh, and joke, and drive Christ out of their hearts, and angels from their presence, by their foolish nonsense. Unprofitable conversation upon the acts of others, small talk about this young man or that girl, withers noble, devotional thoughts and feelings, and drives good and holy desires from the heart, leaving it cold and destitute of true love for God and His truth. 1T 392

With many young ladies the boys are the theme of conversation; with the young men, it is the girls. Out of the abundance of the heart the mouth speaketh. They talk of these subjects upon which their minds mostly run. The recording angel is writing the words of these professed Christian boys and girls. 2T 460

It is the duty of the youth to encourage sobriety. Lightness, jesting, and joking will result in barrenness of soul and the loss of the favor of God. 2T 236

The office is no place for visiting, for a courting spirit, or for amusement or selfishness. All should feel that they are doing work for God's society, talking, jesting, and joking, and angels of God have been driven from the office. 3T 191, 192

CONDUCT FOR YOUNG WOMEN

Young ladies should be reserved and modest. When they walk out, if in health, they do not need the supporting arm of any man... *Testimonies for Students and Workers of our Sanitariums, pg 7*

From the light which the Lord has given me, our sisters should pursue a very different course. They should be more reserved, manifest less boldness, and encourage in themselves shamefacedness and sobriety. Both brethren and sisters indulge in too much jovial talk when in each other's society. Women professing godliness indulge in much jesting, joking, and laughing. This is unbecoming, and grieves the Spirit of God. These exhibitions reveal a lack of true Christian refinement. They do not strengthen the soul in God, but bring great darkness; they drive away the pure, refined, heavenly angels, and bring those who engage in these wrongs down to a low level.

Our sisters should encourage true meekness; they should not be forward, talkative, and bold, but modest and unassuming, slow to speak. They may cherish courteousness. To be kind, tender, pitiful, forgiving, and humble, would be becoming, and well pleasing to God. If they occupy this position, they will not be burdened with undue attention from gentlemen in the church or out. All will feel there is a sacred circle of purity around these God-fearing women, which shields them from any unwarrantable liberties. 2T 455, 456

My sisters, avoid even the appearance of evil. In this fast age, reeking with corruption, you are not safe unless you stand guarded. Virtue and modesty are rare. I appeal to you as followers of Christ, making an exalted profession to cherish the precious, priceless gem of modesty. This will guard virtue.

The slightest insinuations, from whatever source they may come, inviting you to indulge in sin, or to allow the least unwarrantable liberty with your persons, should be resented as the worst of insults to your dignified womanhood. The kiss upon your cheek, at an improper time and place, should lead you to repel the emissary of Satan with disgust Be afraid of anything like this familiarity. Be sure that the least approach to it is evidence of a lascivious mind and a lustful eye. If the least encouragement is given in this direction, if any of the liberties mentioned are tolerated, no better evidence can be given that your mind is not pure and chaste as it should be, and that sin and crime have charms for you. You lower the standard of your dignified, virtuous womanhood, and give unmistakable evidence that a low, brutal, common passion and lust has been suffered to remain alive in your heart, and has never been crucified. 2T 458, 459

Keep clear of the boys. In their society, your temptations become earnest and powerful. Put marriage out of your girl's head. You are in no sense fit for this. You need years of experience before you can be qualified to understand the duties and take up the burdens, of married life. Positively guard your thoughts, your passions, and your affections. Do not degrade these to minister to lust. Elevate them to purity; devote them to God.

You may become a prudent, modest, virtuous girl, but not without earnest effort. You must watch, you must pray, you must meditate, you must investigate your motives and your actions. Closely analyze your feelings and your acts. Would you, in the presence of your Father, perform an impure action? No indeed. But you do this in the presence of your heavenly Father, who is so much more exalted, so holy, so pure. Yes; you corrupt your own body in the presence of the pure, sinless angels, and in the presence of Christ; and you continue to do this irrespective of conscience, irrespective of the light and warnings given you. Remember, a record is made of all your acts. 2T 564

CONDUCT FOR YOUNG MEN

If you, my brother, are allured to unite your life-interest with a young, inexperienced girl, who is really deficient in education in the common, practical, daily duties of life, you make a mistake; but his deficiency is small compared with her ignorance in regard to her duty to God. She has not been destitute of light; she has had religious privileges, and yet she has not felt her wretched sinfulness without Christ. If, in your infatuation, you can repeatedly turn from the prayer-meeting, where God meets with His people, in order to enjoy the society of one who has no love for God, and who sees no attractions in the religious life, how can you expect God to prosper such a union? Be not in haste.

Early marriages should not be encouraged. If either young women or young men have no respect for the claims of God, if they fail to heed the claims which bind them to religion, there will be danger that they will not properly regard the claims of the husband or of the wife. The habit of frequently being in the society of the one of your choice, and that, too, at the sacrifice of religious privileges and of your hours of prayer, is dangerous; you sustain a loss that you cannot afford. The habit of sitting up late a night is customary, but it is not pleasing to God, even if you are both Christians. These untimely hours injure health, unfit the mind for the next day's duties, and have an appearance of evil. My brother, I hope you will have self respect enough to shun this form of courtship. If you have an eye single to the glory of God, you will move with deliberate caution. You will not suffer love-sick sentimentalism to so blind your vision that you cannot discern the high claims that God has upon you as a Christian. 3T 44, 45

INFATUATION AND COURTING

Should you, my brother, go to our College now, as you have planned, I fear for your course there. Your expressed determination to have a lady's company wherever you should go, shows me that you are far from being in a position to be benefitted by going to Battle Creek. The infatuation which is upon you is more Satanic than divine. I do not wish to have you disappointed in regard to Battle Creek. The rules are strict there. No courting is allowed. The school would be worth nothing to students, were they to become entangled in love affairs as you have been. Our College would soon be demoralized. Parents do not send their children to our College or to our Offices, to commence a love-sick, sentimental life, but do be educated in the sciences or to learn the printer's trade. Were the rules so lax that the youth were allowed to become bewildered and infatuated with the society of the opposite sex as you have been for some months past, the object of their going to Battle Creek would be lost. If you cannot put this entirely out of your mind, and go there with the spirit of a learner, and with a purpose to arouse yourself to the most earnest, humble, sincere efforts, praying that you may have a close connection with God, it would be better for you to remain at home. 5T 109

FOR YOUNG MEN AND WOMEN

Angel Records. I have seen an angel standing with scales in his hands, weighing the thoughts and interests of the people of God, especially the young. In one scale were the thoughts and interest tending heavenward; in the other were the thoughts and interests tending to earth. And in this scale were thrown all the reading of story-books, thoughts of dress and show, vanity, pride, etc.

Oh, what a solemn moment! The angels of God standing with scales, weighing the thoughts of His professed children. Those who claim to be dead to the world and alive to God. The scale filled with thoughts of earth, vanity, and pride, quickly went down, notwithstanding weight after weight rolled from the scale. The one with the thoughts and interest tending to heaven went quickly up as the other went down, and oh, how light it was! I can relate this as I saw it, but never can I give the solemn and vivid impression stamped upon my mind, as I saw the angel of God. Said the angel, Can such enter heaven? No, no never. Tell them the hope they now possess in vain, and unless they speedily repent, and obtain salvation, they must perish. 1T 124, 125

One in a Hundred. If the minds of the youth of this age were pure and uncorrupted, the girls might have a softening influence upon the minds and manners of the boys, and the boys, with their stronger, firmer nature, might have a tendency to ennoble and strengthen the character of the girls. But it is a painful fact that there is not one girl in a hundred who is pure-minded, and there is not one boy in a hundred whose morals are untainted. Many who are older have gone to such lengths in dissipation that they are polluted, soul and body; and corruption has taken hold of a large class who pass among men and women as polite gentlemen and beautiful ladies. It is not the time to recommend, as much as possible in the society of one another. The curse of this corrupt age is the absence of true virtue and modestly. 4T 95, 96

Poor deceived souls flatter themselves that they are spiritually minded, especially consecrated, when their religious experience is composed of love-sick sentimentalism more than of purity, true goodness, and humility of soul. 2T 252

You mingle with your religion a romantic, love-sick sentimentalism, which does not elevate, but only lowers. 2T 249

Flirtation with and by Marrieds. The familiarity of married men with married women and with young girls is disgusting in the sight of God and holy angels. The forwardness of young girls in placing themselves in the company of young men, entering into conversation with them, talking common, idle talk, is belittling to womanhood. It lowers them, even in the estimation of those who indulge in such things. There is a positive necessity for reform. All frivolity, all undue attention of men to women, or women to men, must be condemned and discontinued. These things have produced great evil in the world. The first appearance of irregularity in conduct should receive attention; the young should be taught to be frank yet modest in all their associations. *E.G. White in Taylor's Outline Studies, note 8*

BASIS FOR MARRIAGE

True love is a high and holy principle, altogether different in character from that love which is awakened by impulse, and which suddenly dies when severely tested. It is by faithfulness to duty in the parental home that the youth are to prepare themselves for homes of their own. Let them here practice self-denial, and manifest kindness, courtesy, and Christian sympathy. Thus love will be kept warm in the heart, and he who goes out from such a household to stand at the head of a family of his own will know how to promote the happiness of her whom he has chosen as a companion for life. Marriage, instead of being the end of love, will be only its beginning. MYP 466

STANDARDS FOR MARRIAGE: GOD'S APPROVAL

Let those who are contemplating marriage weigh every sentiment and watch every development of character in the one with whom they think to unite their life destiny. Let every step toward a marriage alliance be characterized by modesty, simplicity, sincerity and an earnest purpose to please and honor God. Marriage affects the after life both in this world and in the world to come...If you are blessed with God-fearing parents, seek counsel of them. Open to them your hopes and plans, learn the lessons which their life experiences have taught and you will be saved many a heartache. Above all, make Christ your counselor. Study His word with prayer. MYP 435

If men and women are in the habit of praying twice a day before they contemplate marriage, they should pray four times a day when such a step is anticipated. Marriage is something that will influence and affect your life, both in this world and the world to come. A sincere Christian will not advance his plans in this direction without the knowledge that God approves his course. He will not want to choose for himself, but will feel that God must choose for him. We are not to please ourselves, for Christ pleased not Himself. I would not want to be understood to mean that anyone is to marry one whom he does not love. This would be sin. But fancy and the emotional nature must not be allowed to lead on to ruin. God requires the whole heart, the supreme affections. MYP 460

Those professing to be Christians should not enter the marriage relation until the matter has been carefully and prayerfully considered from an elevated standpoint, to see if God can be glorified by the union. Then they should duly consider the result of every privilege of the marriage relation, and sanctified principle should be the basis of every action. Before increasing their family, they should take into consideration whether God would be glorified or dishonored by their bringing children into the world. They should seek to glorify God by their union from the first, and during every year of their married life. 2T 380

STANDARDS FOR MARRIAGE

Examine carefully to see if your married life would be happy, or inharmonious and wretched. Let the questions be raised, Will this union help me heavenward? Will it increase my love for God? And will it enlarge my sphere of usefulness in this life? If these reflections present no drawback than in the fear of God move forward. MYP 449

Satan is busily engaged in influencing those who are wholly unsuited to each other, to unite their interests. He assaults in this work, for by it he can produce more misery and hopeless woe to the human family than by exercising his skill in any other direction. *2T* 248

Only With Believers. Never should God's people venture upon forbidden ground. Marriage between believers and unbelievers is forbidden by God. But too often the unconverted heart follows its own desires, and marriages unsanctioned by God are formed. MYP 436

But the marriage of Christians with the ungodly is forbidden in the Bible. The Lord's direction is "Be ye not unequally yoked together with unbelievers." MYP 464

Danger of Promises. You may say, "But I have given my promise, and shall I now retract it?" I answer, If you have made a promise contrary to the Scriptures, by all means retract it without delay, and in humility before God repent of the infatuation that led you to make so rash a pledge. Far better to take back such a promise, in the fear of God, than keep it, and thereby dishonor your maker. MYP 441

NO MATCHMAKING

Leave matchmaking and guessing about the marriages of your friends. The marriage relation is holy, but in this degenerate age it covers vileness of every description. It is abused, and has become a crime which now constitutes one of the signs of the last days, even as marriages, managed as they were previous to the flood, were then a crime. Satan is constantly busy to hurry inexperienced youth into a marriage alliance. But the less glory in the marriages which are now taking place, the better. When the sacred nature and the claims of marriage are understood, it will even now be approved of heaven, and the result will be happiness to both parties, and God will be glorified. May the Lord enable you to do the work before you to do. 2T 262

APPENDIX*

A LETTER TO ALUMNI ON UNIVERSITY TRANSITIONS

Dear Friends,   *June 19, 1993. Updated July, 2001

I write for alumni and officials of Andrews and Loma Linda Universities [**AU-LLU**] who asked for true *transition stories*. Some are also inquisitive about my ability substantively represent the Church and its institutions in sharing the College of Medical Evangelists [**CME**] with LLU, and the Potomac [**PU**] and AU university transitions. Yet to give details, my use of the first person will simplify and clarify the questions some of you raise. In any event we give God all the glory, when and where any is deserved.

Although there are many related details, the primary concerns here are (1) the consolidating LLU Medical School's clinical and pre-clinical divisions at Loma Linda, and (2) renaming Potomac University to Andrews, and its relocation from D. C. to Michigan. Since I was deeply involved in both, some ask why we didn't report before. Both instances were too touchy. It wasn't wise to write at the time: At LLU, the Chairman and I opposed the Board's plan to join the divisions in Los Angeles [**LA**] instead of Loma Linda.

Common education factors. Our goal here is *historicity*, not satisfying curiosity. These were important events which have not been accurately nor fully reported. I happened to have training in upgrading and accreditation in higher education, so somehow was drawn into poignant institutional developments of the time. Details in this letter were verified with those intimately involved and understood ambitions and biases of those days, among them: Marion Barnard, M.D., Bernard Briggs, M.D., Mervyn Hardinge, M.D., Charles Hirsch, Ph.D., (then GC school head) and Elder Neal Wilson, veteran of both AU and LLU boards. LLU and AU have common constituents, many common Board members and administrative factors, yet God through His modern prophet Ellen White's [EGW] privided guidance.

Personal history. In 1957-60 as a PU founder, I was caught in its renaming and relocation. 2) If the stories were told much earlier, they may have embarrassed General Conference [GC], AU and LLU men. 3) Yet the perspective of 30 years wipes out casual biases. 4) This is a positive chance to replace rumor with fact. And 5) It should be told personally while the writer can be questioned if necessary.

I started teaching on the junior faculty in Introductory English at Pacific Union College in 1933, then at University of Southern California [USC] where I taught after tours as public school teacher, principal and city superintendent in Southern California and five years as a medical administrative officer in World War II. In 1947 I left USC to lead PUC's graduate program and its accreditation team for state teacher certification. (Our appeal was on the basis of the Bible and Ellen White's books and it brought highest recognition in all areas we requested).

In 1951 we were called to upgrade Japan Junior College to work with God in achieving senior standing, increase enrollment, secure recognition, establish a teacher education curriculum and teacher-student work-study programs consistent with the Spirit of Prophecy, develop it evangelistically and make it debt-free. Then we went to Philippine Union College to strengthen its emerging graduate program. In 1957 Elder E.E. Cossentine and the GC called us to D.C. to help organize PU which became AU. Then to LLU in 1960.

AU transitioned before LLU; yet my Loma Linda background reached back to the early 1930s when my father had a part in the Campus building program. Those were the days when God blessed the old "Co-op Plan" in which preclinical students alternated year round: A month at study on Campus and a month at work in Valley clinical facilities in mentored by the CME staffs, as inspired by EGW in *Medical Ministry [MM]* 81, CT 211, FCE 41, etc. In those days CME led America in national Medical Boards, one year reportedly placing eight of the top ten, including the top man. Clinical years were at the White Memorial and LA County hospitals.

My *professional* introduction to CME came in 1960 after helping start Potomac University [PU], later AU, although I learned medical administration as a World War II Ninth Service Command officer in San Francisco the SF Port of Embarkation, New Guinea (with CME's 47th General Hospital), and in Manila on General MacArthur's staff. That was another series of miracles. GC Education Head Erwin Cossentine asked me to join Elder E. D. Dick, Charles Weniger, William Murdoch, Winton Beaven and Charles Hirsch to organize PU as a union of the SDA Seminary and a new graduate school which was largely teacher education [TE]. We hired three able TE women: Natellka Burrell, Mercedes Dyer and Ruth Murdoch, and also headed the Washington Missionary College (now Columbia Union College) Education Program.

Common Issues. At PU two problems soon emerged, similar to our later experience at Loma Linda: *Name and Location*. First, Dr. Lloyd Blauch, Assistant U. S. Commissioner of Education for Higher Education, told me one day that "Potomac University" had been the name of a defunct diploma mill. At once that started our Board on a search for a new name. The growth of the University was so rapid that the GC voted to move it from its crowded "GC Headquarters Campus". Several Seminary professors wanted to locate it between Takoma Academy and a gulch on the west and surrounded elsewhere by housing and business. Sadly, they had bought or built nearby, perhaps uninformed on how much land a university needs, and possibly unaware of EGW counsel. They wanted PU close to D.C.'s "vast research resources" including the Library of Congress. Yet, other D.C. land was declared "too expensive."

Enter Ellen White. Some knew from Mrs. White and experience and that any SDA university should have much more space than the Seminarians proposed. Dr. Blauch asked, "What is their philosophy?" But he already knew of Ellen White, and answered his own question: "Follow your lady!" I mentioned this to my friend, GC Associate Secretary Paul Bradley, who had been on our Board. He insisted that I tell the upcoming Autumn Council. I agreed only if he asked me from the podium to report on Dr. Blauch. I was part of a closely-knit team including my revered PUC major professor, Dean Charles Weniger, who badly wanted the University as close as possible to the Capitol. To *volunteer* a statement was out of the question.

So Elder Bradley asked. I answered. Administrative rebuttal was instant. But Dr. William Murdoch rose and in his deliberate, majestic, Scottish brogue agreed with

EGW...and Dr. Blauch. The Council voted to search for a non-city site. Board members looked at a number of beauty spots out of town, yet became apparent before the next major meeting that God meant what he said when He told EGW to locate well out of the cities. Into this impasse came Lake Union Conference President Jere Smith and Emmanuel Missionary College [EMC] President Floyd Rittenhouse who offered free land at Berrien Springs, MI and willingness to give up EMC's name. EMC would replace WMC as the University's undergraduate college. The GC concurred with the Board's acceptance of the offer and the name "Andrews University."

God avoids personnel dilemmas. Dr. Rittenhouse, an old friend, and brother of Ruth Murdoch, invited me to Berrien to be dean. Yet Elder Rudy's son-in-law was Dr. Fabian Meier, a beloved professor of education, new from Walla Walla College, already on Campus, and unstained by conflict. It was clear that Elder Rudy wanted Fabian as AU dean of education, so we just asked God to point the way. Dr. Blaunch had for some years said he had an opening at his office, but by divine coincidence I received a phone call from LLU while we all were at a Miami Beach meeting. LLU President Godfrey Anderson and Academic-VP Keld Reynolds urged us, "Come out and get on a *real* team."

I assured them that we were already on a *real* team. But they said LLU needed someone down my "alley," experienced in reorganizing and upgrading higher schools, and invited me to be corporate vice-president, to help reorganize LLU, assist Board Chairman M. V. Campbell, and oversee fund raising. Dorothy unexpectedly became founding director of LLU's Cerebral palsy Center. The president and dean had really wanted to follow EGW in locating the clinical division at Loma Linda instead of taking the two preclinical years to L. A. On that condition I had accepted, knowing success, including freedom from debt, depended on obedience to God. [see Deut 28:1-13]. GC Presidemt Figuhr, urged by Jerry Pettis, my classmate and close friend who had been CME alumni executive, called me in and formally placed the call.

Yet by the time we arrived at LLU in early 1960, 1) the Board was persuaded by LA alumni and GC officer patients to move the pre-clinical Division to LA; 2) LLU's chief fund raiser had written Dr. Anderson strongly that my job should be his, and 3) the president, dean and financial VP felt they must go with the Board.

Leadership vacuum? I asked Elder Campbell about the Board's change of mind: Had he read *Medical Ministry?* He had just read it, and believed it; also *Education* 50 (which says that success in education depends on our fidelity in carrying out the Creator's plan), and Deuteronomy 28: If we "diligently" obey Him, His blessings will overtake us and we will be the head, not the tail. So I knew that to have success in medical education, fund-raising or anything else, we must do as God said through Scripture and EGW. We had seen this plan give PUC high accreditation, upgrade and bring overseas colleges out of debt, and bless AU. Elder Campbell promised full support if I would stay by; we prayed that "things might yet change." He appointed a "Consolidation Committee" to get the facts together, and appeared confident that they eventually would carry the day for Loma Linda. He asked me to present my point of view to the Board despite other LLU officers' agreement to the LA decision. It was a brave gesture for him, for some board members remembered my disruptive AU-location remarks at Autumn Council.

I read to the Board God's explicit conditions for His blessings: Deuteronomy 28 and EGW's *Counsels on Health* visions (pages 156 and 554) on Los Angeles vs Loma Linda:

"By some it was urged that a sanitarium should be built in ...Los Angeles. There was One among us who presented this matter very clearly...He told us that it would be a mistake to establish a sanitarium within the city limits...Loma Linda is in the midst of a very rich district, including three important eities-Redlands, Riverside and San Bernardino. This field [LA] must be worked from Loma Linda, as Boston must be worked from Melrose." And from *Evangelism* 486: "Those who seem to see such great advantages in so doing [building in large cities] are without understanding."

I asked the Board if they thought how we should ask God for qualified personnel, money, necessary accreditation, etc. if we disregard His counsel. During this brief talk I also used the last page of the Patriarchs and Prophets, chapter on the Exodus about faith in face of our own "Red Sea," page 290. At best, interest was mixed: The GC Secretary read the morning newspaper. I was not invited back. But this was God's work, and as usual He eventually had His wise way. This does not suggest that any of the Board or LA boosters were not principled and sincere. An example was Dr. Roger Barnes, my intimate piend and booster from boyhood, who at first was strong for LA, but eventually championed Loma Linda. Vested interests were apparent on both sides.

The quiet team. There were two key factors in decision to consolidate at Loma Linda, of which the first was crucial: 1) Those who favored Loma Linda and 2) those the Board appointed to carry out its decision but who had little to do with the vote. *The first* was a team led by such men as Elder Glen Calkins, Claude Steen M.D., Elder C. L. Bauer, Marvyn Handinge M.D., Ted Halburg M.D. and Bernard Briggs M.D. They brooked no compromise, insisting on Loma Linda, and that the "LA influence" not be brought to the more informal, prevention-oriented LL. Some later said, "Loma Linda won the battle, but LA won the war." LL men preferred the Mayo Clinic method in which the patient receives only one bill, no matter how many specialists treated him, while LLU patients later had many statements. The second team involved Anderson, Reynolds, John Shull (financial VP), David Hinshaw M.D., and other leaders who in their hearts seemed to oppose an LA move, but felt loyal to the Board.

I had known Elder Calkins many years, through my father. He was a retired GC V-P, and encouraged us in our EGW programs abroad. He began calling regularly. Soon he was recruiting alumni, laymen and key Church leaders for counsel on how to counter the change in the Board action to unite at LA. He often called or came to my office or our home. My boss, Elder Campbell, knew how I felt, yet never interfered. GC men like Neal Wilson and Willis Hackett were strong influences favoring EGW and Loma Linda and alumni, like Dr. Owen Parrett and non-LA medical groups such as the Barnard Medical Center in Bakersfield and School of Dentistry Dean Web Prince.

Then there were other men and women on or near the LLU campus, each in his own way, including Ernest Christensen M.D., Lewis George M.D., Herbert Henken M.D., Claran Jesse M.D., Roy Jutzy M.D., Frank Lemon M.D., Ray Mortensen Ph.D., Don Peterson M.D., John Peterson M.D., Gordon Thompson M.D., Richard Walden M.D., Dr. Charles Winters, Tom Zirkle, Sr. M.D., even some from LA, and many missionaries. Some of these people still live and can verify LLU or AU segments of this story, including Mercedes Dyer who shared the AU epoch, and Elder Neal Wilson who shared both.

Elder Calkins worked literally day and night quietly advising and coordinating with the help of Dr. Claude Steen, Pacific Union Conference President C. L. Bauer and others. He was in daily touch with us at LLU by visit, phone or note. A Southern California oil man and car dealer when he joined the Church, he went to PUC, then pastored, but soon became president of the Southeastern California and Pacific Union Conferences, and later GC VP for Inter-America.

Pointing to an upcoming San Francisco [SF] GC meeting, Elder Calkins asked me to publish a letter detailing the Board decision. Although a letter was needed and I was eager enough, I sensed that it would be more effective and ethical if sent by LLU alumni. One active alumnus volunteered to sign as leader, but the consensus was for a leader who was less of an activist. So Dr. Steen, a low-key but widely-loved Fullerton, CA alumnus, assisted by Elder Bauer, became the unanimous choice, and soon had an impressive list of alumni on a letter to GC staffers and others, totaling 17,000 leaders around the world.

Action. Because of the high level of excitement around the issue, it seemed best for me to stay behind when some went to a GC meeting at San Francisco. Dr. Hardinge agreed to keep us informed in the event that stronger representation was needed at the big session. Soon he called, advising a continued low profile, especially for us who, like him, were LLU staffers. He reported that when GC President Elder Figuhr learned of the alumni leaflet, he ordered *Adventist Review* (then *Review and Herald*) Editor Francis Nichol to stop the presses and insert a hastily-written reply to the special issue of the *Review* for the SF session. Elder Nichol obeyed, although he strongly favored Loma Linda.

But Elder Figuhr's hastily-written article backfired, and probaby cost Los Angeles the battle, short as it was on both logic and fact. Haste had made waste, for Elder Figuhr was normally a careful leader. Hardinge's suggestion for patience opened the way for the Steen-Bauer-Calkins group for a point by point answer to Elder F in a second leaflet, formidably documented by sacred counsel and secular fact. It was mailed to the original list. *[For Moore Foundation donors we will send free copies of the two letters until the end of 2002, please send a self-addressed envelope for first-class mail to LLU Letters, Box 1, Camas, WA 98607]* So the final CME/LLU decision came largely from a lay Steen team abetted by such veterans as businessman Clyde Harris, of the LLU Board of Councilors, with guidance from LLU staffers and encouragement from Board members: North Pacific Union President Wayne $criven's remark reportedly crystalized the final vote. Said he, "If we vote LA, we will lose our constituency."

Related factors of possible concern to alumni. Meanwhile other events were underway. We report them with a hope that they might teach lessons which could empower LLU, Andrews and SDA education. This was our rationale for our background remarks early in this letter on obedience is a condition of God's blessings.

Board of Councilors. During LLU events above and with strong support by Campbell, Anderson, Reynolds and Shull, we organized a Board of Councilors [BC], a proven device to obtain otherwise costly counsel and support from highly successful men and women. We patterned our program after the Claremont Colleges. When asked for their advice, such councilors were likely also to become donors, but we reminded the administration that openness to their counsel should be assured before expeditions into their pocketbooks. We also invited spouses; some came to official meetings and nearly all to social occasions. *And no pleas should be made for funds unless the projects were consistent with EGW counsel.*

The founding Board included ARCO Oil Company Property Head Howard Brower; Baton Rouge Cattle, Baker and Oil Man Rex Callicott; Bethlehem, PA Developer Hal

Campbell; Corpus Christi, TX Dentist- Businessman Daniel Coggin; Oregon lumberman Clyde Harris; LLU Builder Larry Havstad; CA lawyer Arthwell Hayton; International Architect John Latimer, Florida Developer Don Loveridge; South Carolina CPA Merrill Patton; Medical media man Jerry Pettis (whom we elected as our first regular chairman); California Manufacturer Harry Schrillo, North Carolina Baker G. G. Welch, and me as founding chairman, *pro tem*.

This board had a powerful influence favoring the move to Loma Linda. Yet some councilors unfortunately began feeling that some LLU leaders reached more for money than counsel. On one occasion a councilor challenged officers: "What do you think we are, a bunch of pink ladies?" The administrators profited by that exchange. Some officers learned that careful stewards check the purposes for their gifts. *The best investments* ***always*** are those in institutions or projects which diligently follow God's plan. When schools recognize this and with fidelity carry out His plan, He blesses above all we ask or think. Otherwise, they may be under a curse. (Deut. 28).

Secular interim. Later, God provided an invitation from the U.S. Office (now Department) of Education [OE]. And Elder Neal Wilson suggested that we could significantly serve the Church there as graduate research and programs officer (masters and doctors) at Washington D.C. Subsequently the President appointed me U.S. Representative to UNESCO. Next was as advanced-study consortium director (Universities of Chicago, Johns Hopkins, Southern Illinois, Stanford, Tulane and Wisconsin). During these secular appointments, the Potomac and Illinois Conferences asked me to associate pastor and pastor in Washington, D.C. and near Chicago.

Common Sense lessons from the secular world. In 1966 when I was with the OE, and after we had received almost identical, costly grant proposals from adjoining universities, the White House authorized me to study cooperation among American colleges and universities. We wanted to showcase sound examples. For instance, Oregon's Willamette University [WU] offered an *undergraduate* forestry degree, but couldn't afford a Master's program. On the East Coast, North Carolina's Duke University had a strong *graduate* forestry program. So the two got together, and soon Willamette forestry students could take three years at WU, move to Duke for their senior year and yet receive a *Willamette* baccalaureate degree, then stay on for a year and obtain a master's from Duke.

On the other hand, Case and Western Reserve Universities, separated only by a fence, had asked us for nearly identical nuclear study grants. Instead we made on joint grant to them. This proved so sound that they merged into Case-Western University, an arrangement that works best when institutions are located adjacent or very near each other. For most however, *cooperation* is the key.

We found over two thousand worthy interinstitutional co-ops that aggregated hundreds of millions of dollars in yearly savings. They included combinations of universities, colleges, libraries, museums, junior colleges, high schools and an almost unlimited choice of agencies and institutions. Genuinely exciting institutional departments, although seldom alert to co-op potential, eagerly responded to the study. Even in the pilot study, the White House would not believe our 90% institutional response, and demanded a second pilot. That one, under close, skeptical supervision, had a response of 91%. So the White House urgently authorized a study all colleges and universities.

The final response was over 91% as compared to the average USOE study response of 29%. Institutional savings are now estimated in many billions of dollars annually and much richer programs. We tell this story in two federal government books, and after a joint Columbia University retreat seminar, we shared authorship of a book, *New Prospects for the Small Liberal Arts College,* published by Columbia Teachers College Press with Victor Frankl, Peter Drucker, and former U. S. Commissioner of Education Earl McGrath, then head of the Columbia University Institute of higher Education.

What, some ask, does this mean for LLU and SDA schools: The stronger institutions were the best cooperators: Harvard, Stanford, Cal-Tech, MIT, Rice, etc. We received hundreds of enthusiastic replies. Ball State and Indiana Universities, about50 miles apart, told how closely they cooperated, and promised much more after a proposed freeway was completed. Yet in the same mail we had word from LLU and La Sierra College in 1967 that they were too far apart to cooperate (20 miles by freeway).

However, in the early 70's, GC officials in a financial dilemma turned the tide. They asked us to replicate the USOE study among North American SDA colleges and universities. They had been duplicating courses and services at unnecessary costs of millions of dollars annually. Some with expensive major departments rarely produced a single major graduate. Although some departments cried "Foul," the GC was firm, suggesting possible subsidy loss for non-cooperators. So a number of major programs-organ, art, math, physics and others who had few if any major students-were set aside as major departments, and interinstitutional cooperative agreements were arranged. Thus a single school of engineering at Walla Walla was stipulated, and pipe organ and other esoteric majors limited to colleges that had major students to justify departmental status.

La Sierra Dean Richard Lewis said this saved La Sierra alone over half a million dollars annually. The GC minimal estimate was more than $3,000,000 yearly saved overall by NAD colleges, yet it produced much richer programs. The only reported violation of the pact was on President Richard Hammill's determination that Andrews also have an engineering curriculum. Finally, he, Walla Walla and the GC compromised with AU's "engineering technology"degree.

A few years later LLU/LSC boards, in a change of mind voted to study consolidation, We strongly advised cooperation instead of merger in view of pride and disagreement on demographic and denominational issues. And Dean Lewis agreed. Yet neither board was persuaded. Consolidation was voted. Soon acrimony largely replaced what cooperation there had been. Eventually trustees of the "united" institution faced reality and returned LSC (now LSU) into their original forms. The situation was largely remedied, although the cost was high in loss of time, money, and pride, uncertainty and emotional stress.

Our schools at all levels can greatly strengthen programs by cooperating with other institutions without violating principle: elementary schools, academies, colleges, museums, libraries, institutes, etc. For example, most of our colleges have now "grown up" and are cooperating with overseas colleges to the relief and convenience of many worthy students and teachers. Extension programs are common across oceans and time zones.

Interinstitutional cooperation has vastly improved among SDA schools in the last quarter century. Most schools freely exchange credit here and abroad. LSC (Now LaSierra University) took the lead. No longer is there sacrifice of credits. Even advanced high schoolers often profit by college classes, often with credit delayed until after high school. We have a letter from senior Harvard Admissions people showing much more generous attitudes than most colleges, including homeschools, particularly to those who balance study with work and service.

Many students are creative in specialties while still in their teens. Recently one of our 18-year-old homeschoolers was invited to present a paper at an Audubon Society world meeting. After finishing an ornithology degree in a cooperative grants program between Harvard, Cornell and Oxford, he was awarded a Rhodes Scholarship at Oxford. He was awarded a Ph.D., and is now teaching at Oxford. Our homeschoolers have special favor at Harvard and LLU, mainly because of their motivation, discipline, creative work and service balance. Four from Kevin Harrington's family have attended LLU, three of them awarded $200,000 MD-Ph.D grants, and at least three or four more of their eleven siblings expect eventually to take Medicine there.

AU awarded graduate credit for Moore Foundation week-long seminars on Home Education by university-qualified personnel. AU also received international recognition for openness to homeschool research in which its faculty and doctoral students substantially shared. PUC, AU and LLU closely work also with Weimar Institute, much like the Willamette-Duke liaison. Others are welcome to share Weimar's now consistent high quality academically, behaviorally and spiritually and the high Church employment record of its graduates, where conferences often give their graduates priority.

Balance of work and service. Whatever the level of education, when study is creative and balanced with work and service, and when students are closely associated with teachers in this activity, the student record in achievement, behavior and sociability far exceeds the norm, so much so that a Harvard senior admissions officer called such students a "luxury". And, well-managed, institutional solvency is certain. For example, Northeastern University in Boston provides education much like old CME did. Most of its students alternate work and study. Those who don't work have the hardest time with their studies, and lower employment prospects upon graduation. Some of our USOE staff at first saw it as a sort of a glorified trade school and gave its grant proposals short shrift. So we selected the highest quality scholars as evaluators and visited its campus. All agreed that it was excellent; so we gave it a multi-million dollar grant.

The California Regional Occupational Program [ROP] has high school students studying half days and working (without pay) half days in local businesses and industries. These half-day students take full work yet are CA's highest average achievers. Oregon recently asked for our help in setting up apprentice programs, German-style. Public school programs, carried out in simple ways with good management and minimal investment—under control of a well-managed school (not private industry) require little or no subsidy, and excel those geared to sports. EGW says, if in doubt, there should be more work than study, for teachers come much closer to students when they work manually with them. Not only are responsibility, promptness and integrity taught, but races and cultures merge. Those two are interested in fostering such God-blessed programs should read EGW's FCE 38-41, CT 211, ED 50, CG 26, 8T, 296 and much, much more. If you need help, write to Box 1, Camas, WA 98706. If you desire copies of book chapters we have done for such universities as Columbia, Maryland, etc., we send them free to donors. E-mail: moorefnd@pacifier.com.

Old-fashioned schools of excellence. Few realize that small schools are usually the best. Studies by states from Alaska, Washington and Idaho across to Tennessee and North Carolina prove that homeschools, properly done, are the best academically, behaviorally and socially. For a copy of the MOORE FORMULA [MF] and reasons why, send a SASE to MF, Box 1, Camas, WA 98607. It describes a study-work-service balance where students learn how to earn a living and develop self-worth and self-control instead of beating another team. It also avoids peer dependence, the social cancer of our age that gives the back of the hand to family values, splits homes and gives us insecure, asocial, amoral, church-scorning kids.

But the bottom line in nearly all our educational dilemmas today is the early entrance of our children into institutional life. Hands-down research, including widely-acknowledged findings by LLU and AU scholars, has proven the certainty of scientists at Stanford and Cal-Berkeley to Columbia, Cornell, Tufts and others in the East that ages 11 to 13 are by far the best for school entrance age and the pressures of formal study. No wonder EGW said that all children should if possible be educated in a home school "until maturity," much like the maturity of ancient Israel with girls considered mature at 12 and boys at 13. If you are interested in a brief documented article we wrote for *Reader's Digest* or the *Journal of School Health,* ask for either, free. But please avoid danger of wrong addressing by sending us a self-addressed envelope, preferably with postage, unless you are a donor.

Today the extremely inexpensive, low-stress homeschool is possible to any normal parent who is warm and responsive, regardless of the parents' educational level. In many states homeschool parents like the idea of an umbrella or mothering school where their students can go for such studies as welding, woodwork, art or band, and will gladly pay. One such small Canadian church school mothered more than 500 homeschools. Public schools, too. On the other hand, like Greece and Rome of old where early-schooled children paid little attention to their death-house parents, today we are reaping history. *The earlier you institutionalize your child, the earlier he will institutionalize you!*

For most of the last 30 years, I have served as CEO and president or chairman of two Church-oriented non-profit research foundations. An elderly couple whom we had helped with a complex land deal surprised us with a gift of $750,000 in cash and lake-view property. We took this to the GC for counsel, and organized a nonprofit research foundation which was not bound by church-state restrictions. Its board included two GC vice-presidents and the GC treasurer. This, for example, permitted us to accept funds offered by both Senate and House of Congress for early schooling research.

God then surprised us again when He used the *Reader's Digest's* 52,000,000 readers world-wide and turned our Ellen White-inspired research into the world's largest alternative school movement—old-fashioned American *homeschooling*. She had written that every child should be taught in a homeschool until maturity and if that could not be done, to teach them in a church school run as nearly as possible like a well-run homeschool. [CG26, 8T226] You will soon see how this strengthens the story.

Learning from laymen and research. We have proven that if we all 1) read Scripture and EGW as if our eternal life depended upon them, 2) seek lay counsel much more urgently and comprehensively, 3) place more laymen on key committees, and (4) *listen to them,* we will increase both in prosperity and in power, and greatly reduce behavior problems and subsidy needs in our institutions and homes. So if we want our institutions to be the head and not the tail, we donate personally to those who build and operate by obeying God *diligently*. If we don't, we invite God's curses. Dorothy and I read Deuteronomy 28 as though our prosperity and eternal life depended on it. For they do, in every school's balance and every hospital's size, staff and salaries; and likewise at home.

SUMMARY. Sixty-five years of teaching, administration and research have taught us that history, research and common sense thoroughly support divine counsel from Scripture and EGW. *All* those schools who locate and operate, with much later school entrance ages and balanced programs combining *at least* as much teacher-led manual work as study, as God directs, are highly successful (FE 41, CT 211, etc). SDA and non-SDA schools prove this from Coast to Coast. To help our educational institutions at all levels, let's pray that they "with fidelity carry out the Creator's plan." ED 50. As the motto says, that Henry Martin gave me to hang in my office: "Before all else fails, read the Instructions." The good steward places his assets on that basis, and receives miracle blessings, not His wrath, His curses nor institutional demise.

—Raymond S. Moore, Chairman/CEO, The Moore Foundation

THE HANDS OF GOD

I lift my eyes to nail-scarred Hands
That guide the stars through space,
That shape the graceful form of shore
And put the isle in place.

I see the Hands that form the phlox
And understand the rose,
That know just how to tuck the flowers
To sleep at twilight's close.

The Hands that light the moon by night
And fire the sun by day
Are selfsame Hands that give the glow
To fire-fly's tiny ray.

I see the touch of Fingertips
That tailor mountain tops
Lend feather touch to eyelash,
'Ere sorrow's tear should drop

At sunset I see brush in Hands
That deftly tints the cloud;
At bedside through the darkest night
They grieve to lift the shroud.

Those Hands hold in their palms the seas
That stretch from pole to pole.
Yet form with wisdom infinite
The outlines of a soul.

In faith I see the Hands of God
Through heaven's open door
And find myself in His embrace,
His Hands forevermore.

—RSM

120